UNDERSTANDING AND LOVING A PERSON WITH

POST-TRAUMATIC STRESS DISORDER

UNDERSTANDING AND LOVING A PERSON WITH

POST-TRAUMATIC STRESS DISORDER

*Biblical and Practical Wisdom
to Build Empathy, Preserve Boundaries,
and Show Compassion*

STEPHEN ARTERBURN, M.Ed.
AND BECKY JOHNSON

DAVID C COOK

transforming lives together

UNDERSTANDING AND LOVING A PERSON WITH
POST-TRAUMATIC STRESS DISORDER
Published by David C Cook
4050 Lee Vance Drive
Colorado Springs, CO 80918 U.S.A.

David C Cook U.K., Kingsway Communications
Eastbourne, East Sussex BN23 6NT, England

The graphic circle C logo is a registered trademark of David C Cook.

The website addresses recommended throughout this book are offered as a resource to you. These websites are not intended in any way to be or imply an endorsement on the part of David C Cook, nor do we vouch for their content.

Details in some stories have been changed to protect the identities of the persons involved.

LCCN 2017918223
ISBN 978-1-4347-1057-4
eISBN 978-0-8307-7229-2

© 2018 Stephen Arterburn
The Author is represented by and this book is published in association with the literary agency of WordServe Literary Group, Ltd., www.wordserveliterary.com.

Cover Design: Amy Konyndyk

Printed in the United States of America
First Edition 2018

1 2 3 4 5 6 7 8 9 10

012918

Contents

Introduction

I don't have to imagine what it is like to believe in someone, to believe a person has my best interests in mind, to believe a person is in control of the lusts and desires of the heart, only to be traumatized by the betrayal, adultery, lies, and deception that occurred during the affair that shattered my world. That trauma ripped through me like nothing I had ever experienced before. But it did not end there. I was blamed for the affair. I was told that if I had been different, if I had been better, it would not have happened. But that was not enough either. Eventually, I was accused of being the one who caused the most pain in the aftermath of the affair I don't want to remember.

It was Dr. Sheri Keffer who knew my story, saw the impact of what had happened, and told me I was still suffering from the aftermath of that trauma. She suggested I see a trauma therapist to deal specifically with the betrayal trauma and the affliction of ongoing pain caused by someone who had no awareness of their personal defects and the need to change from the inside out. I continue to do the work I need to do with that specialist. It takes time to resolve and heal the destruction caused by trauma.

I wanted this topic and this book to be part of the Arterburn Wellness Series because those who love me have been hurtful and helpful, and I don't think they know the impact of what they have said or done. Your reading this book is a dream come true for me because I know it will be a great handbook for helping someone who has experienced trauma. It has everything you need to act as a healing force in the life of someone who is in deep unresolved pain or who is reacting to the past rather than responding appropriately to the present. Thank you for wanting to be helpful to someone who really needs you to be that way.

Perhaps the person you care about needs to see a specialist like I did. This book could help you aid your loved one to see the need and motivate him or her to get that level of care. It also may provide you with enough healing and helpful options that you determine a specialist is not needed. I know it will show you a path and a process for you to maintain your own sanity and stability in the wake of some radical post-trauma reactions. It really is designed to make your life better, not just help the person you love have a better life.

There was a time when the phrase "post-traumatic stress disorder," or "PTSD," only referred to soldiers returning from a brutal war who were triggered into a reaction as if they were still on the battlefield. "Shell shock" was another way of referring to a combat neurosis that interfered with a person's ability to function normally. The most common example depicted in numerous movies is when people hear a loud bang, such as a car backfiring or an exploding firework, and think or feel as though someone were firing a gun at them. They will either cower in fear or attack the nearest person. That is a real form of PTSD, but there are so many variations and other forms of it that it is easy to not recognize the heart of the matter.

This book will help you see PTSD for what it is and how it is affecting you and the one you love. It will help you respond rather than react. It will lead you on a path that initiates healing and resolution and restoration for the one you love. It is love that motivates people to get out of themselves and get into another person's pain. I am so glad you are a person who loves enough to want to help someone live a better life outside of the impact of his or her trauma.

—Stephen Arterburn

CHAPTER ONE

How Can I Help My Loved One with PTSD?

> Everyone has a right to have a future that is not dictated by the past.
>
> Karen Saakvitne, *The Trauma-Informed Toolkit*

Ayden walked into the master bathroom where his wife of eight years was blow-drying her hair. But Bella didn't hear him come in, and when she turned and suddenly saw him standing near her, it startled her so badly that she jumped about six inches off the floor, dropped the blow-dryer, and began screaming.

"I'm so sorry!" Ayden said. "I tried to let you know I was coming into the room, but you couldn't see or hear me."

After the screaming subsided, Bella fell into Ayden's arms, trembling and weeping. It would take her most of the evening to calm herself and "come back into her right mind," as she called the process of reorienting herself to the reality of the present.

A few years earlier, Bella had been diagnosed with post-traumatic stress disorder (PTSD). And Ayden was learning how to live with, comfort, love, and encourage someone with a brain that had been deeply affected by past trauma.

"I try to be so careful about not accidentally startling my wife, who suffers from PTSD related to trauma from abuse in her past," Ayden shared. "Bella's PTSD was not from one major traumatic episode, as some PTSD survivors' experience. Her brand of PTSD is complex, having resulted from decades of surviving a confusing, painful relationship. There were multilayered instances of abuse that happened without any consistent pattern she could nail down, so she could not figure out how to avoid it. She never knew when the abuser from her past would be kind or belittling, attentive or abandoning. It was intermittent and random. This left her with a nervous system set on high alert. Even after she was safe in a calm, loving marriage to me, the symptoms continued."

In Bella's case, the intermittent and uncontrollable nature of the abuse left her feeling particularly vulnerable and hypervigilant— her nervous system was stuck on high alert.

Why Doesn't My Loved One Feel Safe?
Why Symptoms *Now*?

Some people find it hard to comprehend that PTSD symptoms are often at their worst when life is great again (or great for the first time). In fact, many people's PTSD symptoms do not even materialize until they are safe, after all danger has passed. We have all heard of brave soldiers who muster adrenaline-stoked courage and stamina to survive the horrors of war in a foreign land but become hypervigilant and jumpy or emotionally paralyzed when home. Back stateside, a soldier is finally safe enough to experience feelings that had to be ignored or tamped down in order to survive a battle in progress. Though the public often associates PTSD with shell-shocked war veterans, PTSD is much more widespread, and it is also often underdiagnosed. Anyone who has undergone any kind of trauma, whether sudden and severe (like a car accident or severe injury), long term and intermittent (like relational abuse or cancer that goes in and out of remission), or some combination thereof, can experience PTSD.

People who have been triggered into reliving a negative memory or sensation from that memory often report feeling completely out of control. "PTSD is not something that my wife can control intellectually. Her brain and body are simply reacting—on autopilot—to a trigger, an incident that brings old trauma memories to the surface," Ayden explains.

I can attest to the truth of Bella's story because I also suffer from PTSD. And yes, it is a real thing—not an excuse, not a "fad diagnosis," not a figment of the imagination. Trauma changes us, and trauma that had to be "put on hold" in order to survive a situation—without a safe place to process and let it go at the time—changes the brain in ways that neuroscientists can see in before-and-after brain scans. Your loved one can improve, but it may take a long time (depending on the type and severity and length of the trauma endured), and his or her brain may always be set on a higher alert status than before the trauma experience.

However, I am here to offer you some real, tangible help, hope, and encouragement. Though I am occasionally triggered and have a PTSD episode, I have discovered several methods that calm my overanxious brain. I now startle less easily and don't jump as high or yell as loudly when someone surprises me. As an aside, I have lost count of how many store clerks I have accidentally scared when they came up to me and asked, "May I help you?" Startled, I would jump and scream, and then they would jump and scream. Fun times in the grocery store aisles!

I have learned to access the logical part of my brain (prefrontal cortex) and am less controlled by the hypervigilant, fearful parts (the hippocampus, basal ganglia, and amygdala) when something triggers a painful memory or feeling. I don't react as badly, and I recover much more quickly. If I am practicing good self-care, I find it much easier to roll with the occasional PTSD punches. And I owe much of my progress to the persistent, patient, loving heart of my current husband. In addition, my work as a researcher and writer for therapists and doctors has given me an inside perspective into practical ways to help myself (ones that really work!) and others.

The Blessing of a Reparative Partner

I am so thankful for my good husband, who has stayed right by my side, determined to give me new memories of safety, faithfulness, love, and responsiveness to take the place of those memories involving danger, betrayal, contempt, and abandonment from a past dysfunctional marriage. He has given me the gift of what are sometimes called "reparative moments"—healing responses—that pour over old emotional wounds like a soothing balm.

In this book, I want to share how you too can be part of your loved one's healing journey and how you can support his or her efforts to recover his or her life after trauma. This is a subject near and dear to my heart, and I am thankful for the opportunity to share what I have learned about what PTSD is, how it happens, how it changes the brain, and how to heal from its effects. I'll also share what family members and friends can do to support a loved one's journey toward emotional healing.

In years past, before I experienced some of the symptoms of PTSD for myself, I am not sure I would have believed someone else describing the whole odd phenomenon to me. But now I know, not only from my personal experience but also from studying what happens to human bodies after trauma, that PTSD is a very real thing.

Some counselors believe that PTSD is, in its most simplified form, grief that got stopped, stalled, or shelved in order to handle a present crisis. Counselors, family, and friends can help by understanding that their loved one with PTSD has suffered a great loss, or perhaps multiple losses, and never got to talk through what happened sufficiently (in the presence of a compassionate listener) or cry the tears that got stopped up and stored away. You can't do her healing for her, but you can support her efforts. And I will show you how to do so in coming chapters.

I will also help you take care of yourself so that you don't get washed away in the tide of your loved one's PTSD triggers. Researchers have shown that those who live with a person with severe PTSD also show signs of increased anxiety. The same is true for people who live with someone who is in a major depression (which can go along with PTSD); they may find themselves spiraling into depressive feelings as well. Most spouses of those with PTSD end up walking on eggshells to some degree, never knowing when their mates will be triggered and blow up or shut down. The good news is, you'll discover that almost everything I suggest to help calm your beloved PTSD survivor will also help you to remain calm. This book is a twofer: use the ideas within for yourself even as you share them with your mate.

What You Can and Can't Do to Help

The purpose of this book is not for you or your loved one to go back in time and wallow around in painful memories. In fact, it can be risky for anyone who is not a professional to delve deeply into trauma memories with someone who has PTSD. You can inadvertently trigger emotions too strong for the average layperson to deal with—an experience that can feel a bit like opening Pandora's box. A surgeon never begins open-heart surgery without a clear plan to monitor the process, stitch the patient back up, and offer pain-reducing therapies during the recovery phase. Someone who has specialized training in PTSD knows how to listen to trauma memories compassionately while also monitoring and treating his or her client for undue stress during verbal recall exercises. If the trauma was severe and is very hard for your loved one to talk about, it is best to let a professional be the one to hear the details of the memories so your loved one can process them at a safe and soothing pace.

However, your loved one may want to share some past trauma memory with you at some point. If so, I will give you specific ways to listen to that memory, monitor his or her reactions, and respond in wise and healing ways.

There's much you can do to support your loved one, whether he is in therapy for his issues right now or he isn't ready for or doesn't want to get professional help. I can help you understand some of the changes that may have occurred in your loved one's brain during past trauma and how to respond in ways that are helpful instead of hurtful, healing instead of potentially demeaning or even damaging. We are all more compassionate and patient when we understand the story behind others' behavior. When someone you love experiences a PTSD trigger, her reaction can be puzzling, concerning, and in extreme instances, even frightening. But when you (1) understand what is happening inside her mind and body when triggered and (2) have a variety of concrete practical ideas to try, along with soothing phrases to say and activities to do with your loved one, you won't feel quite as helpless or hopeless.

Practical emotional tools empower us all.

In short, I am here to coach and companion you, as you companion your loved one through the journey of healing from PTSD. I believe I can help you because I know how my husband and other counselors have helped me. Once again, you can't "fix" another person; it is his job to prioritize healing his own life. But you can let her know that you are with her for the long haul as she works on her own emotional health. And you can be a part of a reparative moment when something you say or do touches a person's heart and pours the balm of love and acceptance over a painful memory or deep wound.

Here is one example of just such a moment. In a former marriage, when I would recognize a certain demeaning tone in my ex-husband's voice, it would signal, "A bad experience is about to happen! Danger! Danger!" I learned to react to this tone of voice in one of three ways, which I refer to now as the three Fs: (1) flight (pack my bags to leave), (2) fight (brace to defend myself or verbally attack him), or (3) freeze (go into a detached state of numbness, retreating to a faraway place of self-protection). In my current marriage to a mature, emotionally healthy man—especially in the first few months and years—I would get triggered by any slightly negative tone (or even something as small as a sigh of disappointment), and rather than pausing to talk things out with Greg, I would go into autopilot and respond with one of the three Fs.

Then one day, Greg said to me, very thoughtfully and tenderly, "Becky, when you feel hurt or angry or afraid, you don't have to leave; I am not going anywhere. You never need to raise your voice; I am always going to listen. And you don't have to freeze or tense up or withdraw; I'll give you any space you need, and I am here to hold you when you are ready for a warm embrace."

I still melt every time I remember those words in that poignant moment in our first year of marriage.

For years now, I have shared Greg's compassionate, healing words with many young couples over kitchen-table conversations when they have come to us for help in their marriages. It never fails to bring a tear to the woman's eyes and to show young husbands how to, as Greg calls it, "shepherd a wounded woman's heart."

Somehow Greg knew exactly the right thing to say to me, and that night I eventually put down my suitcase, then curled up in his loving arms and wept pent-up tears from long-ago years, tears I'd never felt safe to shed before. These tears came and went, unbidden, for a couple of days. Even when I was not consciously thinking about trauma memories—even when I was just washing dishes or folding laundry—my entire body was at work releasing pain from a former life. Bessel van der Kolk wrote a classic book on PTSD, *The Body Keeps the Score: Brain, Mind, and Body in the Treatment of Trauma*, in which he presents what researchers have learned about PTSD—namely, that it is much more than an affliction of the mind. Every cell in our bodies remembers trauma, even trauma that we may not consciously recall. So in addition to talk therapy, therapies that engage the whole body—such as a healing massage, or even a long soak in a hot tub—can be very helpful. Healing involves brain work, soul work, and body work.

Over time, Greg's love, wise understanding, and healing embrace broke a decades-old dam of pain and allowed the hurt behind the barrier to flow. My marriage has offered many reparative experiences, overlaying profoundly meaningful and healing moments on top of painful ones. In time, the old hurtful scenes have begun to fade, like washed-out watercolors, as Greg continues to paint new and more vivid scenes wherein I am both loved and cherished. My ability to trust that he will show up and love me—and has eyes for me only, forever—grows moment by moment, day by day, month by month, year by year. I went from a nervous, insecure newlywed afraid he would change his mind about loving me or desire another woman and leave me to a wife who is confident and secure in her husband's steadfast love and rock-solid faithfulness. I have learned to trust a man again. It was no easy task. But my man has earned every drop of trust I have in him and our happy and healthy marriage.

What Greg did for me, you can do for someone you love who battles PTSD. You can't do it alone; he has to participate in the healing and seek out professional help. And you can't fix every single bad memory, as much as you would love to do just that. This is God's task—way beyond the scope of your job description. But you can be a compassionate companion to your loved one as she pilgrims from trauma to healing, however long that journey might take. At the core of someone who suffers from PTSD is a person who longs to know that he is not alone—that someone sees his pain, cares for his heart, and will stay the course until he finds his way out of the dark.

Author Note: First, because reading lots of details about specific traumas that others have suffered can trigger a PTSD episode in the reader, I will be pretty generic about types of traumas, focusing mostly on the feelings left in the wake of abuse or a traumatic incident and then on ways to comfort, soothe, and heal from the kinds of memories that interfere with the joy of the present.

Second, because every individual experiences PTSD in a unique way, some ideas in this book will work beautifully for you and your loved one, while others … not so much. Most people find that healing comes from a variety of sources as they put together their own plate of helpful resources. Use this book like a menu and try what sounds most appealing. Keep what is helpful and toss what isn't. Go back and try one or two other ideas when you get stuck.

Finally, this book may contain ideas that will help a parent who has a child suffering from some form of trauma or PTSD, but the category of children with trauma is beyond the scope of my focus and is a specialized area of its own. I will, however, list some resources for parents of traumatized children at the end of the book.

CHAPTER TWO

PTSD—Yes, It's a Real Thing

SIGNS AND SYMPTOMS

When we understand what PTSD is, we can begin helping our loved ones. But since we can't see PTSD the way we can see a broken bone, how do we know it is real?

First, therapists use a standard psychological litmus test to assess their clients. The American Psychiatric Association says in the *DSM-V*[1] that diagnosis of PTSD requires "exposure to an event that involved or held the threat of death, violence or serious injury."[2] Exposure can happen in many ways. For instance, you might

---

1   *DSM-V* is the standard shorthand for *The Diagnostic and Statistical Manual of Mental Disorders*, fifth edition. It is used as a classification and diagnostic tool for psychiatric diagnosis.

2   James A. Athanasou, *Encountering Personal Injury: Medical, Educational, Vocational and Psychosocial Perspectives on Disability* (Netherlands: Sense Publishers, 2016), 103.

- witness the traumatic event in person,
- learn that someone close to you experienced or was threatened by the traumatic event, or
- be repeatedly exposed to graphic details of traumatic events (e.g., if you are a first responder to the scene of traumatic events).

After a traumatic event, you might experience one or more of the following signs or symptoms:

1. You relive experiences of the traumatic event, such as having distressing images and memories
2. You have upsetting dreams about the traumatic event
3. You experience flashbacks as if you were experiencing the traumatic event again
4. You experience ongoing or severe emotional distress or physical symptoms if something reminds you of the traumatic event

In addition, for more than one month after the traumatic event, you may

- try to avoid situations or things that remind you of the traumatic event;
- not remember important parts of the traumatic event;
- view yourself, others, and the world in a negative way;
- lose interest in activities you used to enjoy and feel detached from family and friends;

- feel a sense of emotional numbness, feel irritable, or have angry or violent outbursts;
- engage in dangerous or self-destructive behavior;
- feel as if you're constantly on guard or alert for signs of danger and startle easily; or
- have trouble sleeping or concentrating.

Your symptoms can cause significant distress in your life or interfere with your ability to go about your normal daily tasks.

For children younger than six years old, signs and symptoms may include

- reenacting the traumatic event or aspects of the traumatic event through play or
- experiencing frightening dreams that might include aspects of the traumatic event.

Regardless of its source, trauma contains three common elements:

1. It was unexpected.
2. The person was unprepared.
3. There was nothing the person could do to stop it from happening.

Simply put, many people feel like traumatic events are beyond their control. A car swerves headlong into your lane. An argumentative husband suddenly goes into a controlling rage and puts his wife in a chokehold. A grenade is thrown into a soldier's path. It is not just the event that determines whether something is traumatic but the individual's experience of the event and the meaning he or she gives to it. Those who feel supported after the event (through family, friends, spiritual connections, etc.) and have a chance to talk about and process the incident are often able to integrate the experience into their lives, like they do any other experience.

We all go through painful, disappointing, and disruptive experiences. We didn't get a coveted part in a play. Our beach vacation is ruined by nonstop rain. We missed an important catch in a baseball game. A beloved grandparent passes away. These events make us feel sad, become disappointed, and even feel grief, but we are highly unlikely to develop PTSD because these instances were not life-threatening; we didn't feel as though we might not survive or that our basic needs for safety and love were at risk. In all of the aforementioned cases, we may feel temporarily depressed and blue for a while. But we aren't triggered into a detached emotional state and don't suffer months of night terrors when we watch a play or see a baseball game or go on another beach vacation. Generally, we have people who rally around us to help us cope with and process sorrow and disappointment and grief. Our brains and bodies process pain, loss, and sorrow in healthy and normal ways. Trauma becomes PTSD when severe pain gets "stuck in the brain" and doesn't have a chance to go through the normal processes that help us recover. PTSD is like a compressed spring of pain in the brain—pain that was never fully expressed or released in the presence of compassion and safety. It just sits there, coiled but never fully released, causing your loved one repeated episodes of tension and anxiety and fear.

What PTSD Looks Like Up Close and Personal

Therapists and other mental health professionals usually focus on three elements when diagnosing PTSD. First, people with PTSD repeatedly relive memories of the traumatic experience. These memories are triggered by images, smells, sounds, words, tones, or any number of things. Once triggered, people with PTSD can go into an extreme physiological state and experience psychological stress. They may tremble, cry, feel terror or rage, or feel paralyzed (the "deer-in-headlights" reaction). Once the PTSD episode is over, people may feel shame or self-blame at their inability to control their reactions following a trigger.

Second, those with PTSD will try to avoid anything that reminds them of the trauma. Sometimes you'll see emotional numbing or sense that a person is detached from the present moment. Some people may not be able to experience pleasure as they once did, and many withdraw from engaging with others and with life in general.

Third, people with PTSD seem to be stuck in state of high alert: they may be hypervigilant, on edge and irritable, have problems remembering and concentrating, suffer from insomnia, and startle easily. Hyperarousal causes traumatized people to become easily distressed by minor irritations. Their perceptions confuse the present and traumatic past, so they may react to everyday frustrations as if they were traumatic events.

The core issue of PTSD is that painful emotions related to a past trauma keep returning, cause unhealthy reactions, and do not fade with time.

From my own experience, here is a fairly long list of the various ways I have personally experienced PTSD. I hope it will help you see what PTSD symptoms can look like in your loved one, and I hope it does so in a way that is a bit more personal than a clinical list.

- *Repetitive nightmares.* These dreams force sufferers to relive aspects of former trauma.
- *Crying for hours.* After being triggered by something in the present that connected to a painful memory, my eyes would "leak tears" as I moved about the day, washing dishes and folding laundry. Drip, drip, drip, drip. I now believe that I was crying tears in the safety of the present that I was not allowed/able to cry while in the thick of surviving my chronic crisis in the past.
- *Transference.* This means that someone in my present, even a safe and loving person, who said or did something that reminded me—in any small way—of things leading up to past trauma would sometimes morph into the former abuser in my mind's eye. We will talk more about this later, but if you are married to someone with PTSD, you may feel like you are suffering for the evil that someone else inflicted on your beloved or like you have a target on your back if you inadvertently say or do something that triggers a bad memory.

- *Fight or flight.* Someone who has been in a traumatic relationship or a frightening experience may respond in one of
  three ways to perceived danger: (1) he may respond with
  anger that is out of proportion to the actual event, (2) he
  may physically try to run away or hide, or (3) he may shut
  down emotionally and go numb for a while. I will share
  some ways to help your mate calm himself and get reori-
  ented into reality after he's been triggered into the fear-
  based fight-or-flight mode.
- *Uncontrollable trembling.* After suffering a fright, animals in
  nature will often tremble in order to discharge the adrenaline built up during a crisis. Any soldier on the front lines
  would know exactly what I'm referring to. Have you ever
  had something terrify you out of the blue? A close call in a
  car accident? The fear of having lost sight of a small child?
  Seeing your kid go down on the football field after a rough
  tackle? You probably had a surge of energy to make it
  through the event. But once all was well, did you feel your
  legs turn to Jell-O? Did you need to sit down because you
  were trembling? Even though your loved one may not have
  actually gone through a real crisis, if she was triggered, it
  feels to her body and brain *as if* she had relived a true crisis.
  Her body will respond accordingly, often by trembling, the
  body's automatic way of discharging adrenaline buildup.
- *Dissociation.* Has your mind ever been so caught up in a
  problem, memory, or worry that you forgot what you were
  doing and where you were? Perhaps you were worried about
  a loved one going through a tough time and drove right

past your exit on the highway? This is a small example of dissociating. During a PTSD episode, this is even more pronounced. An ex-soldier may be triggered by a loud noise from a backfiring car engine or even fireworks, and his brain and body could be instantly transported back to an explosion and a terrifying, unfolding, and danger-filled trauma. When this happens to ex-soldiers, every cell in their bodies and brains makes them feel as though they are back in the war zone—back in crisis. Their bodies produce the same adrenaline they would feel during a real attack. They lose touch with the reality of where they are and what they are doing in the real world. This is why therapists will use a technique called "grounding" to help PTSD clients orient themselves in current time and space. We'll see more of this too in chapters to come.

- *Recurring intrusive stress memories.* Whether the trauma was one major event (like 9/11) or a series of events that lasted over a period of years (abuse or neglect), a few vivid and painful memories often seem to get stuck in the person with PTSD's brain. These can manifest in the form of flashback scenes replaying themselves in your loved one's mind. Or she may mentally hear a voice saying belittling or contemptuous words that would, in the past, precipitate violence or abandonment. These "stuck thoughts" can play on an endless loop on the brain's trauma memory channel. These images and words can be so painful to visualize, rehear, and relive that even the bravest of souls may contemplate suicide to end the horror in their own minds. Many turn to drugs and alcohol to temporarily numb the terror within. But there is a way to break up these stuck memories so they can more easily be reconciled in your loved one's mind. In fact, there are many ways to do this. I will share them in coming chapters.

- *Numbness / paralyzed emotions.* Men who have been through trauma often react to post-traumatic stress by shutting down their emotions. This was, in fact, a survival skill in whatever war zone they experienced—be it a tangible battlefield or a war zone of the emotional kind at home. People can use detachment as a means to survive and navigate a crisis. You may notice your loved one is emotionally detached if he has a faraway look in his eyes or if his responses seem stunted or in some way inappropriate to the moment. He may say, "I love you," but his eyes and expression don't reflect any real feeling. Or he may say "I'm okay; I'm fine" after an emotionally troubling event, but you sense this is a robotic response that doesn't derive from deep or genuine feeling.

- *Shutting down.* Commonly, people who are confronted with a trigger try to physically escape to a safe place. They may curl up in the fetal position or sit in a closet or anywhere they can lock a door, even though they are in no physical danger from you or anyone else. Their bodies are trying to create a circle of safety and get away from remembered danger. They may be unable to form words or coherent sentences. Their eyes may have a faraway look in them, as if they are not fully present. This is a sign of being

ungrounded. Emotionally, they aren't fully there. Again,
you may sense anger or fear directed toward you, anger or
fear that is misplaced and unfair. I will offer suggestions for
dealing with this in chapters to come.

- *Increased fear/anxiety in certain situations.* For people with
  PTSD, certain places, sounds, and even smells can trigger
  a feeling of panic. If your loved one was in an accident, he
  or she may have a hard time driving for a while. Survivors
  of 9/11 sometimes have an odd sense of doom on beautiful
  autumn days because the weather was incredibly beautiful on September 11, 2001—before all hell broke loose.
  Personally, I will begin to tremble and react to any kind
  of belittling tone from anyone, even on television, which
  made the presidential election of 2016 a year of almost
  daily media-induced PTSD triggers. In my situation,
  belittling and dismissive words preceded the worst abuses.
  Perceived threats of abandonment can also trigger deep fear
  of rejection if rejection and abandonment were common
  experiences in someone's past. Crowds. Noises. Smells.
  Basements. Raised voices. Slammed doors—anything that
  reminds your loved one of a time when he felt powerless
  against oncoming attacks or abandonment can trigger a
  negative automatic response in his nervous system.

- *Exaggerated startle response.* Many people with PTSD startle
  more easily than others, their bodies reacting in an exaggerated way to a sudden noise or a person coming into a room
  unnoticed. I am one of those people. If Greg touches me
  to wake me up or enters the room when I don't hear him

coming, I will feel a rush of terror and scream out loud. Every time. We can laugh about it now, and I calm down quickly, but my startle response is still intense and may not ever totally settle down. Interestingly, this startle response wasn't a part of my life before or during the actual traumatizing years. It is a post-trauma response—part of the change that occurred in my brain after enduring years of a dysfunctional marriage.

This list of symptoms is admittedly subjective and internal. However, there's a newer, less subjective, and very interesting way to see if your loved one has PTSD. It is like looking at a bone with an X-ray to see if it is broken. Dr. Daniel Amen, who is a pioneering psychiatrist and brain disorder specialist and good friend of mine, gave me a brain scan as part of my "information gathering" for a book that I was writing with Dr. Earl Henslin, his colleague. Dr. Amen believes it is a crime that we diagnose people with various brain maladies and mood imbalances without actually taking a look under the hood— that is, at the brain via SPECT scans. The following is the story of how a brain scan helped me discover that I had PTSD.[3]

PTSD and the Brain

I walked into the Amen Clinic a little apprehensive of what having a brain scan would feel like but even more worried about what my brain would look like and what story it would tell Dr. Henslin and Dr. Amen. First, I was given a small amount of a radioactive

3   I have rewritten and adapted the material in the following section for this book from Henslin's *This Is Your Brain on Joy* (220–24).

isotope through an injection; it would help my brain's activity become visible on the scan. It was truly painless, and the isotope is harmless. Next, I took a short attention test in the form of a computer memory game. Finally, it was time for the scan. I lay still with just the top of my head inside a big scanner (it looked very similar to an MRI machine) for about twenty minutes while it turned and made loud clicks as it captured photos of my brain.

Afterward, I went to the doctor's office and sat at a small round table where I was soon joined by both Dr. Henslin and Dr. Amen. To my great relief, the first words out of Dr. Amen's mouth were, "Becky, you have a beautiful brain!" Indeed, it looked like a smooth tie-dyed ball of Play-Doh on the scan.

"When the image is smooth like that," he continued, "without ripples or dents, it means that you have a good blood flow throughout your brain. Structurally, your brain is very healthy—no signs of anything toxic or concussions or other brain injuries." I was enormously relieved by this news, as Alzheimer's runs in my family, and I tend to be forgetful and ditzy and daydreamy. It was as if Dr. Amen read my mind at this point. "Earl," he said, "do you see that small indention in Becky's prefrontal cortex area?"

Dr. Henslin nodded. "Yes. It's not very deep, but how were the results of her attention test?"

Dr. Amen smiled and said, "Terrible." He explained that the harder I tried to concentrate, the more blood moved out of my prefrontal cortex rather than flowing into it—a classic sign of attention deficit disorder (ADD).

Putting together the results of the scan, plus some earlier intake information and the results of my attention test, I was diagnosed with what Dr. Amen calls "inattentive ADD." Dr. Amen groups types of ADD into seven categories, and unsurprisingly, mine was basically the "ditzy, daydreaming, forgetful" personality. It explained a lot.

Looking at the next scan, Dr. Amen showed me what was called an "active SPECT scan." Rather than showing the overall blood flow in and around the brain, it showed brain activity. If an area of the brain had too many red or white patches on the scan, then it could represent overfunctioning, or instances when the brain was "firing too hot," as Dr. Henslin would sometimes explain it. This scan showed a lot more red-hot activity than I had expected to see. "Do you have any past traumas that you struggle with?" Dr. Amen asked as he looked over the scan.

I confessed that I suffered from what Greg and I would call "episodes"—all of them relating to trauma memories from my previous marriage. I told the doctors that for a few years, I'd had nightmares in which I would be faced with and try to escape from a frightening memory. In those dreams, I would become paralyzed and unable to scream for help. Usually I was fine during daytime hours, and my experience of life (particularly since my second marriage) was always joyful and peaceful—unless I was somehow "triggered" by a person or event that reminded me of past pain. Then I would react by shutting down or trying to flee. It was the oddest thing, even to me—the person it was happening to! I also told them about an experience when Greg and I were on the patio in our backyard and one of our guests began speaking in a nega-tive tone to his wife. I didn't say a word, but I immediately stood up, went inside the house, and locked the door behind me. My whole body shaking, I walked upstairs robotically and went into my bedroom, locking the door. Then I went into the bathroom, locking *that* door as well. Then I just sat there and tried to breathe and recover from whatever had just happened to my mind and body.

What happened was that I had been triggered by a tone of voice that reminded me of confusing and painful experiences that I had once endured on a fairly regular basis in what felt like a past life. However, my body was reexperiencing what I'd wanted to forget and went, on autopilot, into "shut-down-and-get-outta-there" mode.

"You have a scan that shows the classic diamond pattern of over-activity in the areas associated with PTSD," Dr. Amen said gently. "You've probably got some trauma memories here that got 'stuck' in your brain's neural system."

Dr. Amen went on to explain that on a SPECT scan, the pat-tern of PTSD typically reveals overactivity in multiple regions of the brain—often referred to as the "diamond-plus pattern." Over-activity in three areas are typical: (1) the limbic system (an area associated with depression and grief, located at the bottom of the diamond), (2) the basal ganglia (areas associated with emotions of fear or worry, occupying the left and right sides of the diamond pattern), and (3) the cingulate (an area near the top of the dia-mond indicating that there are "stuck" thoughts). Taken together, you can see that the ways we experience PTSD often involve mild to severe sad or depressive feelings coupled with anxiety and fear, which are in turn linked to a brain that obsesses over memories that cause sadness and fear. This high activity also tends to keep the brain functioning on overdrive, increasing anxiety and irritability and interfering with sleep. It is as if the brain is always "waiting for terror"—on high alert to protect the body and psyche from another real or imagined attack.

I felt both sad and relieved. At least there was a name for what had been happening to me: post-traumatic stress. Dr. Amen then shared that brain scans can show radical improvement after sessions with a professional therapist who is trained in how to treat PTSD. He also suggested some supplements that could be helpful and emphasized the need for quality nutrition, exercise, and regular relaxation or prayer/meditation activities.

When Dr. Amen first discovered that there was a certain pattern of brain activity associated with PTSD, the practice of using brain scans as a diagnostic tool was innovative and controversial. Today, researchers have published dozens of studies about the way trauma alters the brain. Neuroscientists in China have recently discovered that brain structures change as PTSD progresses. For example, the scientists found that a "shrinking left superior parietal lobule was distinctly linked to PTSD." In November 2013, researchers performed the first study using imaging to identify and compare specific brain regions of individuals who had experienced similar traumas and later developed PTSD.[4]

People of all ages can have PTSD. However, some factors may make you more likely to develop PTSD after a traumatic event:

---

4   Christopher Bergland, "The Neuroscience of Post-Traumatic Stress Disorder," *Psychology Today*, *The Athlete's Way* (blog), November 5, 2013, www.psychologytoday.com/blog/the-athletes-way/201311/the-neuroscience-post-traumatic-stress-disorder.

- experiencing trauma earlier in life, including childhood abuse or neglect;
- having a job that increases your risk of being exposed to traumatic events, such as military personnel and first responders;
- having a genetic predisposition to anxiety or depression;
- lacking a good support system of family and friends; and
- having biological relatives with mental health problems, including PTSD or depression.[5]

All these facts are fascinating, but the bottom line is this: What now? What can a person whose brain has been changed by past trauma do to get better?

The good news is that the brain *can* change for the better—with help. It can repair itself or exercise, stretch, and grow other regions so that you become a more balanced person. Neurologists use the word *neuroplasticity* to describe how the brain continues to grow and change, even into adulthood. More and more scientists are discovering ways to stimulate positive growth and changes in the brain, leading to a calmer and happier life for people suffering from PTSD or other debilitating disorders. Some of the scientists refer to this process as "post-traumatic growth." I like that concept and point of view, and I will discuss this idea more toward the end of this book.

---

5   Bergland, "Neuroscience of Post-Traumatic Stress Disorder."

Triggers

One of the most common and major hallmarks of PTSD is what we refer to as a "trigger," or any event in the present that instantly links to a trauma from the past. Triggers can be words, sights, smells, songs, or tones of voice—in other words, almost anything that reminds someone with PTSD of a former trauma or abuser. People can be triggered consciously or be completely unaware of what their specific trigger is. But something is registered—a line from an old song on the radio, for example—that causes what I call a PTSD episode, which is what psychiatrists refer to as an "intrusive reaction." Some feeling or thought intrudes into a person's brain, and he or she is suddenly thrust—emotionally and physically—into bad memories and unpleasant sensations. It's like traveling back in time to the worst possible moments in your life and being forced to repeat them again and again. You can imagine how this can make life a living hell, especially if those memories and feelings are excruciating and you feel powerless to stop them. It is no wonder that those with severe trauma experiences might turn to alcohol or drugs that numb the mind to emotional pain and replace it with substance-induced euphoria. Of course, we all know where addictions can lead, and that picture is not pretty. Learning how to prevent, cope with, or lessen the impact of triggers is a vital (and teachable) skill for those with PTSD.

Types of PTSD and Their Causes

You may be wondering if there is more than one type of PTSD. I can tell you that yes, indeed there is. Psychiatrists now divide PTSD into two major categories: type I and type II.

When someone has either experienced or witnessed a single traumatic and unanticipated event, type I PTSD is more likely to occur. These are called "critical incidents," and they can be anything from an assault to a natural disaster, a violent crime, or an accident. Some of the common symptoms of type I PTSD are

- intrusive, repeated disturbing memories or dreams of the stressful experience;
- suddenly feeling as though you are reliving the traumatic experience;
- feeling upset and having stress reactions when something reminds you of the event (e.g., pounding heart, trouble breathing, trembling, sweating, feeling tearful);
- avoiding anything that might remind you of or trigger painful memories;
- loss of innocence or trust that the world is safe, and feeling anger and wanting to blame someone for this loss;
- depressive symptoms, such as losing interest in things you used to enjoy and feeling numb to emotions of love, connection, and joy;
- feelings of being detached or cut off from others;
- being irritable or having angry outbursts;

- feeling hyperalert or watchful on some level for any potential danger or signs of impending danger;
- being easily startled;
- having difficulty concentrating (even putting thoughts or to-do lists together and following them is difficult); and
- trouble falling asleep or staying asleep.

Type II PTSD is also sometimes called "complex PTSD" because … well, it's more complicated and pervasive and can take longer to treat. This type of PTSD is more likely to occur if the trauma happened early in your loved one's life, was prolonged, and was interpersonal. If your loved one lived with someone who was in any way abusive and the situation was chronic and long lasting, he or she may have this type of PTSD. Some symptoms of complex PTSD include

- inability to regulate moods, especially anger;
- difficulty staying fully present, particularly when triggered;
- feelings of shame or guilt or a sense of abandonment;
- having a mixed bag of internal messages, including anger at the abuser or belief that the abuse was somehow deserved or even warranted;
- difficulty trusting others—sometimes withdrawing, sometimes looking for someone to rescue them, sometimes looking for someone else to rescue;
- feelings of despair and hopelessness, coupled with a struggle to find meaning, look forward to a happier future, or find faith;

- tendency to abuse substances as a way of coping with severe emotional pain; and
- deliberate self-harm.

In addition, your loved one may have some combination of both types of PTSD, especially if he or she survived a chronically abusive/neglectful relationship as well as a catastrophic event (or several). In my experience, these often go together because chronic daily drama in a home sometimes yields periodic high-octane drama that can quickly become a vivid, shocking, catastrophic memory. An alcoholic parent may be intermittently angry and irrational at home and then perhaps cause a traumatic car accident while intoxicated. Or he or she may get arrested. Or the children may have been taken to foster care. Or worse. In these cases, a child may grow up with chronic and intermittent trauma accompanied by sharp, clear, intense trauma memories and later display symptoms associated with both types of PTSD.

PTSD Facts

- An estimated 70 percent of adults in the United States have experienced a traumatic event at least once in their lives, and up to 20 percent of these people go on to develop PTSD.
- An estimated 5 percent of Americans—more than thirteen million people—have PTSD at any given time.

- Approximately 8 percent of all adults—one of thirteen people in this country—will develop PTSD during their lifetimes.
- An estimated one out of ten women will get PTSD at some time in their lives. Women are about twice as likely as men to develop PTSD.[6]

Now that we know what PTSD looks like and what some of its causes are, the big question remains: How do we help someone we love who suffers from past trauma? It begins with defining our role—what we can do, and what we cannot do—to help someone with PTSD. And that's what we'll explore in the next chapter.

6   "Post Traumatic Stress Disorder Fact Sheet," Sidran Institute, accessed September 1, 2017, www.sidran.org/resources/for-survivors-and-loved-ones/post-traumatic-stress-disorder-fact-sheet/.

CHAPTER THREE

Becoming a Compassionate Companion

> Hospitality is not to change people, but to offer them space where change can take place.
>
> Henri J. M. Nouwen, *Reaching Out*

In this chapter, I want to share with you how to show compassionate care and empathy toward your loved one with PTSD. This chapter contains a wide variety of practical ideas. Even though some of them may sound odd—or even quirky—there is good science and research behind everything I've suggested. There is a lot of information, but don't get overwhelmed. Remember to use this book like a menu: read all that is offered, pick one or two ideas that you think might be helpful, and try them out. If they work, great. If not, reread the ideas at a later date and, in the meantime, try another. Somewhere in here, you will find a few ideas that will help you handle your loved one's PTSD meltdowns while maintaining your own mental balance.

In the sections that follow, I will talk about the importance of self-care, which is about giving *yourself* compassion in a variety of ways. You really must prioritize your own mental balance because (1) you are worth it—you are God's precious child—and (2) you can be an example of peace and happiness and a healing force in your own family and beyond.

Fixing versus Companioning

> Self-compassion is defined as "kindness directed toward the self." At its core, trauma affects a person's capacity to be self-compassionate, so trauma recovery is about nurturing and growing that ability.
>
> Klinic Community Health Care,
> *The Trauma-Informed Toolkit*

The verb *treat* (as in to care for, improve) comes from the Latin word for "to drag." And the word *patient* means "passive long-term sufferer." So when you think of "treating a patient," the original word picture isn't very pretty. You visualize dragging some passive, suffering person to try to get him some form of help.

This is exactly what you don't want to do, and you don't want to even hint at doing this for (or to) your loved one. I much prefer the term *companion*, which is made up of the Latin words *com*, which means "with," and *panis*, which means "bread." This is a word picture of sharing a meal with someone who is a friend and an equal. Grief counselor and author Alan Wolfelt teaches the art of companioning others through pain in his books and classes. He describes the image of companioning as one that resembles "sitting at a table together, being present to one another, sharing, communing, abiding in the fellowship of hospitality."[7]

---

7   Alan Wolfelt, "The Companioning Philosophy of Grief Care: Being Present to Pain," TAPS, December 1, 2016, www.taps.org/articles/2016/companioningphilosophy.

That's a far cry from dragging a passive patient to care.

Companioning someone through grief, pain, or PTSD is not about assessing, analyzing, or resolving. It is not a "teaching" situation. It is about being totally present. It is about observing, honoring, and bearing witness to another's pain. So when we companion someone in any kind of pain, we come to her as an equal, sharing an experience together, rather than as someone seeking to guide her. We come to hear her stories, to listen deeply, to honor and be gentle with what we hear. Some therapists use the term "catch and cradle" as a visual example of how to do this. We listen to the stories of those in pain (catch the stories) and then we cradle their stories in our arms, we say tender and loving words to the person who is sharing her heart—treating her stories as tenderly as we might treat an infant. We may say things like, "That must have been so painful. I hear the hurt in your voice, and I'm so sorry you experienced this." Or we may ask questions like, "So when that person you loved walked out the door and slammed it behind them, how did you feel inside?"

It takes a lot of vulnerability for someone with PTSD to share even a small part of a traumatic experience. Being fully attentive and tender as you listen is usually more curative than attempting to present any advice on how to "get over it."

When someone honors you by taking the risk to share his heart with you, listen attentively. Ask questions. If he can articulate an answer, try to help him get what he needs to feel even a little bit better. Every person is unique. Some people love a phone call; some hate talking on the phone—it drains them. Some enjoy going to a movie with a friend; others prefer chatting over a glass of wine at dinner. Some release stress through hiking in nature; others decompress through quiet alone time on a porch swing with a favorite book. Some want to talk about light, angst-free subjects; others crave raw, real, honest conversations that wrestle with reality and its meaning. Some want to pore over and discuss questions about God, such as "Where was God in this tragedy? In this excruciating pain? What is He thinking? What is He up to?" Observe what seems to comfort your friend or loved one, and if you can't figure out what seems to soothe him, don't be afraid to simply … ask. "What is helpful for you these days?" or "What feels hurtful?" are usually very welcome questions if asked with kindness and sincerity.

Another important insight when companioning others is that wounded people seldom tell "the whole story" of their traumas all at once. They tend to want to share small bits or aspects of it. To delve into the whole of it feels overwhelming. Babette Rothschild provides a great visual metaphor for the way trauma is released safely, in small bits, over time: "The experience of emotional over-whelm is similar to that of a shaken bottle of soda. Inside the bottle is a tremendous amount of pressure. The safest way to release the pressure is to open and close the cap in a slow, cautious, and intentional manner so as to prevent an explosion."[8]

If and when your loved one wants to share a piece of his story, make sure that you don't gloss over or belittle it or give glib advice. Now is not the time to say something like, "Okay, but that was *then* and this is *now*. It's time to move on!" Christians may rush their loved one with PTSD into forgiving her perpetrator before the groundwork of compassion, self-nurturing, and

---

8   Babette Rothschild, "Trauma Essentials for Making Therapy Safer" (paper, Winnipeg, Manitoba, 2010).

understanding is laid. Forgiveness is not, as many Christians mistakenly believe, usually the first step in healing from the trauma of a painful relationship. In fact, it is often the final step, and it may take weeks, months, or years before someone who has been severely traumatized is strong enough to offer forgiveness. Think of it this way: if your loved one stumbled into the emergency room covered with blood from gaping wounds, would you say, "Wow! Have you forgiven the person who did this to you?" No! You'd tend to his wounds, and if he needed surgery and rest to recover, you'd lovingly, graciously give him time and space to do that. Only when your loved one has been a long time on the path to recovery would you ask if he might be ready to think about forgiving the person who hurt him. And in my opinion, it is best if you let your loved one who was wronged and hurt bring up that subject on his own time and in his own way. You can't push someone to forgive. The time to forgive tends to open up and unfold naturally once your loved one is healthier and happier and more centered in life.

If your loved one trusts you to share even a piece of her trauma story, treat it as a sacred honor. Stop what you are doing, pause the TV, put down the cell phone. Pay attention. Make eye contact. Touch her hand if she is receptive to that. When she stops talking, say, "Thank you for trusting me with this, for honoring me with your story." Then ask, "Is there anything more you'd like to share?" When your loved one has unburdened all she wants to share at that point, say something like, "I'm so sorry this happened to you. You are a precious person. You did nothing to deserve this. Life is often so unfair. I wish I could fix it or go back in time and change it. But I am here for you now, and I will stay with you as you go through this journey." If this person cries or trembles, ask if she wants you to hug her. And a Kleenex and a glass of water may also be appreciated.

If you are married to the person with PTSD, you may ask if you can lie down and spoon with him or her: that is a very comforting and healing posture for couples. If you are a man holding your wife like this in your arms, you may try a gentle rocking motion, one you would use to calm a child. This can be helpful and soothing to the brain and the body. After a time, ask gently, "What do you need right now?" If she doesn't know, you might suggest a few simple, calming activities such as a hot bubble bath, a walk, a bite to eat, or a movie.

Tap into Empathy

Let's face it: life is difficult.

It's also miraculous and wonderful, but nobody gets out of this life without experiencing some pain, and most of us have been through some sort of trauma. Although your painful memory or experience may not have blossomed into full-blown PTSD, tapping into your own painful memories and how they affect your reactions today is a great place to build empathy for your spouse with PTSD.

Though Jack does not have full-blown or invasive PTSD like his wife, Emily (an abuse survivor), he does have some childhood trauma memories that affect him, and certain situations trigger him to react in predictable, protective ways. When Jack was a boy, his father suddenly and shockingly left the family after an affair with another woman. Jack's idyllic home, happy existence, and comforting neighborhood were suddenly … gone. He ended up in a cheap apartment, the only child still at home, with a mother who was going through horrific grief. He remembers that the apartment was infested with ants, and to this day, if he sees a line of ants in the house, he is flooded with feelings of disgust and grief. Ants are a trigger to the memories of a happy childhood that got lost in the trauma of divorce. In addition, his mother dated some real losers in the aftermath of her divorce. There was a lot of drama and yelling in the apartment. Jack reacted by shutting down and losing himself in the hobbies of collecting and organizing: stamps, coins, sports pages, matchbook covers, and more. It doesn't take a therapist to see that Jack found comfort in anything he could order and control while the world around him was in chaos. To this day, when he is under stress, Emily will find him organizing drawers and cleaning out a closet (which, she admits with a grin, comes in kind of handy). Also, his stomach churns when he hears people argue, even on TV or in movies. "Jack can handle the graphic violence of *Braveheart*, or war movies, but he can't abide a scene where family members are angry and yelling at each other," Emily shared.

By understanding his own trauma memories and the aftermath of them on his adult life, Jack has tapped into a way of empathizing with Emily when her PTSD is triggered. By tapping into his memories of feeling helpless and trapped as a boy and by shutting out trauma by distracting himself with absorbing activities, he experiences empathy when Emily is not fully emotionally present. "Jack knows my reactions are in response to some long-ago trauma. He has somehow learned to speak to my deepest fears rather than respond to my presenting behavior. It's taken time and practice, but he has learned how to be a compassionate companion who knows how to help me calm down while also calming himself—reminding himself that my reactions may have nothing to do with a current reality but are about my reliving an old bad memory."

Think back on your life and take note of any painful memories or even mildly traumatic experiences and consider how they affect your reactions or relationships today. Use this as a springboard to understand how something that happened a long time ago can trigger automatic negative reactions in your loved one. The difference between what you experience and what someone with full-blown PTSD experiences is simply a matter of severity and degree—and also the genetic makeup of his or her brain, along with any changes in brain patterns after trauma.

Grounding: Help Them Feel Safe

You can't read very far into the literature on PTSD without encountering the word *grounding*. Therapists use grounding as a technique to help a person experiencing stress feel safe and fully present again—instead of floating off into his or her negative memories, lost in another time and place. We can use grounding to orient ourselves in our present reality. It is becoming more consciously aware of our bodies; it's the feeling of having both feet on the ground, fully present and aware of our surroundings versus the feeling of being "lost in space" inside our own heads. If you've ever gotten lost in your thoughts—whether from a negative or a positive experience—you realize what it is like to become less aware of your body. It's easy to run into people or even bump into a wall or forget to do the most basic things like eat or drink or move into a more comfortable position.

When your loved one is triggered, you may see a far-off look in his eyes. He may be almost immobilized. Anything you can do to help him get grounded again, to become aware of his body, may help ease him out of the PTSD episode. In fact, people can be so kidnapped by their own thoughts and feelings that they look like they're in a trance.

A simple way to help bring a person "down," as it were, from trauma memories is to help her engage all her senses. Think about the five senses of taste, touch, smell, sight, and hearing. Use the sense of touch by holding her hand or having her grab hold of the arms of the chair she is sitting in. That can help ground someone in the present. I personally love getting into a hot bath because the warmth of the water surrounding my skin is instantly reorienting and calming. A soft, heated blanket is a big comfort in winter, and the warmth around me helps connect me to the sensations in my body. If your loved one is open to a massage, either by you or by a professional massage therapist, this can be wonderfully grounding and comforting after a PTSD episode. Pets are also so calming and helpful to those of us with PTSD that I have dedicated a section to them in coming pages. But for now, suffice it to say that petting or holding a beloved cat or dog can lower blood pressure and signal the release of all those feel-good, calming hormones.

Engage taste by offering a glass of cold water or mug of hot tea. The digestive system may be on "lockdown" when people with PTSD are triggered, so they may not be able to eat. But drinking water or hot tea is often helpful. Chewing soft ice chips or gum engages the large muscles of the jaw, and that is not only helpful in grounding but soothing to the frazzled brain.

Engage your loved one's sight by taking him to a calming and beautiful place, outside in nature if possible. I have had some people tell me that going someplace bright and cheerful, with lots of things to look at, helps them calm down. Places like Target with its bright spaces and happy colors or a thrift store with lots of things to look at can be fun for those who find comfort in seeing lots of eye candy. For others, these places can be overwhelming. They prefer to be somewhere clean and serene. If your guy is into sports, suggest a trip to a big sporting goods store. One of my friends, who was going through a divorce and feeling like everything was out of order in his life, found comfort in simply walking through the Container Store, where everything had a function and purpose and a place (this same man also loved stamp collecting as a hobby when he was going through trauma and its aftereffects). Beauty in nature is nearly always healing in and of itself and calming to most of us. If it is too cold (or hot) to go outside, just sitting by a big picture window and looking out at nature can also be helpful. Sunshine, in any form, is its own healing force; it affects the pineal gland and also delivers comforting warmth and vitamin D to the body.

Don't forget the value of scents! Smells can also be powerfully centering and calming. You've likely heard about essential oils and the effect they can have on alertness or relaxation. I love to keep an oil that relaxes me (lavender) and one that energizes me (peppermint or lemon) in a bottle with me. I put a drop or two on my hands, rub them together, create a minitent with my hands, and breathe in and out slowly. (Some strong essential oils need to be blended with a carrier oil to dilute them before putting directly on the skin or they can cause irritation. Check the instructions!) Both the smell of the oil and the slow breathing is calming and focusing for me.

You can use earthy smells when focusing on "grounding." In fact, essential oils or combinations that promote grounding or clarity are especially helpful, and often these oils will have a woodsy or forest-like scent to them: spruce, juniper, cedar, fir, and pine oils are often part of the mix. I happen to love strong, happy smells like citrus or peppermint as well—oils that add clarity, focus, and a sense of joy. If you are in the car, try rubbing an oil on your hand and then holding your hand up to the vent to diffuse the scent. One mother tells me she uses this trick on car trips with the kids when they get cranky. You can even find oils in small roll-on bottles so you can quickly and easily access relief.

Not into oils? Find out what smells are a comfort to your mate. Many love the aroma of coffee or cinnamon. Put on a pot of coffee or go to a coffee shop. Sprinkle some cinnamon or vanilla into a little pot of water and put it on simmer. You can also add apple or orange peel if you like. The sense of smell, like music, bypasses logic and goes straight to the "feeling" part of the brain. Without a word, it can change a mood.

Speaking of music, many people with PTSD find that certain types of music will ground and soothe them. Find out what music calms your loved one and make a playlist. Some people produce audio recordings specifically designed to calm a stressed brain, using soft music and directed instructions by a narrator that facilitate progressive relaxation. Sounds such as birds chirping or the rush of a river or even the soft whir of a rotating fan can also help.

In addition to engaging the five senses, try to involve your loved one in any kind of movement to help ground her and reorient her to the present. The exercise of walking (or swimming or running) can burn off the adrenaline buildup related to a PTSD episode. Any kind of rhythmic movement like rocking or swinging is very helpful, and we'll talk more about this in later chapters.

You can also create a safe place in your home for your loved one to go to when he is feeling stressed. Encourage (or help) him to create a comforting corner filled with things that relax his senses: a rocking chair or some sort of swinging chair is perfect because that rhythmic motion calms stress. Consider a candle, a place to play music, a soft blanket, access to soothing drink or snacks, and nearness to a window that looks out to a calming scene.

Other Helps

You may also want to check with a doctor or naturopath about medications, herbs, amino acids, or supplements that can help calm a PTSD attack, particularly if your loved one feels panicky. The downside to most antianxiety drugs is that many are also highly addictive. I recommend trying everything else first to take the basic level of anxiety down a notch or two. Supplements such as GABA or theanine (from green tea) can be helpful.

Be sure to check into a good omega-3 fish oil. Brain expert Dr. Daniel Amen recommends this supplement for everyone who wants a healthy, balanced brain. It appears to be helpful—sometimes miraculously so—for almost all mood disorders. In some cases, your loved one might need a large dose to get the therapeutic result. Dr. Amen also recommends that everyone have their vitamin D levels checked because most people are deficient in this vitamin and it affects our moods. Check with your health practitioner, preferably someone well versed in natural supplements and their effects on brain and mood balance. Also keep in mind that exercise has proven to be as helpful as most antidepressants without any of the common negative side effects.

Our bodies are incredibly unique, and you and your spouse may have to experiment a bit to find just the right combination of supplements. If these natural substances don't work, your loved one can ask his or her physician to prescribe the least-addictive medication in the lowest dosage and take it only when absolutely needed—before an anxiety or stress-producing event, for example, or when he or she feels a panic attack coming on.

Getting Your Ph.D. in a Person with PTSD

When my husband and I used to teach classes for young married couples, we would tell them to try to get a Ph.D. in each other. In other words, we asked them to study the other person through observation, the way one might study a rare animal in the rain forest. We wanted them to get curious about their spouses' habits and emotions and to notice what makes them happy, what makes them blue, what calms them. In a similar way, you can do this for your loved one with PTSD. Become a "noticer" and observe what happens when he has good days or when he handles a trigger with less reactivity. Ask, "What was he doing? What was in his environment?" Experiment by re-creating these activities and surroundings as best you can for your beloved, especially when she is going through a rough PTSD patch. Curiosity is a much more interesting and calming way to approach relationships than having set expectations and becoming frustrated.

And while you are at it, get a Ph.D. in yourself as well. Know what activities and thoughts are most soothing for you. People are unique; each one is like a plant that blooms best under certain conditions. A cactus needs lots of sun and very little water, while other plants need shade and a lot of moisture. What conditions help your loved one bloom, to be at his best and most balanced self? And what conditions help you feel the same way? Note these observations, create lists, and then do more of what works to foster calm and good moods and less of what doesn't.

Conversation with a Triggered Loved One

When I am with someone who is suddenly triggered and overreacts with anger and seems lost in her own thoughts, I have found it best avoid the topic that she is stressed about and instead speak to the part of her that is like a wounded child. So instead of asking, "What did that clerk say that ticked you off so badly?" I might say, "I am so sorry that this hurt you so much. You are deserving of love and kindness. What do you need right now to help you feel maybe just a little better? Want to go for a walk or take a hot bath? What is your body telling you that you need right now?" In this way, you don't dismiss the pain he is feeling, but you are helping him reorient from ranting, looping thoughts in his head to physical ways to comfort his body. I have two adult sons who have had some trauma in their pasts, and they will both call me when they feel triggered. And they usually feel better after we talk. Why?

First, I allow them to rant or say what they need to say, but I stay calm and keep my voice positive and soothing. I tell them how sorry I am that they had such a bad experience and acknowledge how much it obviously upset them. Then I may say, "What are you doing right now? Where are you?" And the million-dollar question: "What do you need to do right now to help you feel a little bit better?" This stops the negative loop and inserts a question that invokes reasoning skills and problem solving. It engages them in thoughts of self-soothing activities, and the intensity in their voices starts to fade. When I feel as though they are truly calm, I will sometimes share a funny story or a positive quote or scripture verse or a memory of how one of their ancestors overcame a similar problem. This ends our conversation on a positive note. Also, I don't take their reactive anger personally. I know they have been triggered. They don't need me to solve the problem; they need me to be a soothing, safe place.

One word about this: you can be understanding when someone needs you to listen to his or her pain, anger, or frustration, but you can also have boundaries. If the anger begins to be directed toward you, if you begin to feel like you are taking on his or her stress, or if this person calls too often or rants too much, you may need to be honest and say, "I am so sorry you are having a bad day. I want to listen and be understanding, but right now, I am feeling stressed by this conversation. Can we both take a break, maybe take a walk, and try again when we both feel calm?" If he can't respond rationally, it is okay to hang up the phone and do whatever you need to do for yourself. When he is calm, you might also recommend a therapist or a book or an audio recording or podcast or group therapy program that could be of help. In this way, you can steer him to help that can "follow him home" when you are not around.

Reassure and Encourage

One of the most encouraging things you can say to a loved one who is feeling disoriented or like an "emotional basket case" is, "I love you. Your brain is in a lot of pain right now. But listen to me: *you are not your trauma.* The real you will come through this and be stronger for it." In fact, the word *encourage* comes from the idea of putting courage into someone else. You can help your loved one feel more courageous with your reassurances.

People who are triggered and stuck in that space can say things that feel way over the top or wildly negative. Remind yourself often that it's the "trauma" speaking and has nothing to do with you, especially if you know they are experiencing overwhelming emotion after a trigger.

One thing that has helped separate "me" from "my trauma" was when I saw my own PTSD patterns on that brain scan. I no longer think, "I am crazy"; I think, "My brain is experiencing an emotional overload. What I feel right now may not necessarily be real." Then I work at things that I know calm my brain. There is a "me" and there is "my brain," and after I saw my own brain scan, my ability to understand and have compassion for myself when my emotions are causing a meltdown has helped me realize two things: (1) the overwhelming feelings are temporary and are distorting reality and (2) the real "me" is not my trauma, and once the trauma memory has passed and my emotions have settled, I will feel like myself again.

In some relaxed moment, you might want to tell your loved one, "I know the real you is the person you are when your brain is in balance. I know you don't feel yourself when you are triggered and reacting to that, and I understand. You are flooded with emotions that hurt. Can you tell me what helps when you are overwhelmed? What can I do to help? What can you do to help yourself?"

I have also learned that I am much more susceptible to triggers and PTSD episodes if I am tired, hungry, or frustrated. Eating well, taking supplements, getting fresh air and sunshine, learning something new, being around beauty—all these help me stay more balanced. I have also learned that I "bloom best" when I have a lot of margin to my life, when I don't fill my calendar or to-do list to the brim, and also when I have a good balance of solitude versus being around people. People who already have a brain that is wired to be more anxious are most vulnerable to PTSD. I have found that many of us with PTSD fit into the category of what Elaine Aron calls "highly sensitive people."[9] I think this is because those who are highly sensitive tend to have brains that run a little more "hot" with anxiety (genetically) and therefore are more apt to develop PTSD after trauma.

---

9   Elaine Aron, *The Highly Sensitive Person* (New York: Citadel, 1996). Traits of highly sensitive people can be found in Ann Morin, "9 Common Traits of Highly Sensitive People," *Psychology Today*, *What Mentally Strong People Don't Do* (blog), www.psychologytoday.com/blog/what-mentally-strong -people-dont-do/201609/9-traits-highly-sensitive-people.

Try to offer as much grace as you can to others struggling with a brain that is currently out of balance. My husband, God bless him, has learned to take things less personally, knowing "this mood shall pass." He speaks to my true needs (to feel safe, to feel loved, to not be abandoned) and ignores some of the crazy things I may say when in a full-blown PTSD meltdown after being triggered. He's got his Ph.D. in me.

Your Body in Balance

Here's another thing I learned about my brain, something I believe is true of many people with PTSD. I tend to wake up feeling a little bit sad and negative. This worried me until I realized that my brain hasn't had any nutrition while I was sleeping. Once I have had coffee and some protein, my mood brightens dramatically. So when I wake up, I tell myself, "Becky, don't believe anything you are thinking. Wait to think, and don't have any meaningful conversations until you have fed your brain." In the same way, you can learn to read your loved one's moods and also observe what she needs to nourish her brain and feel better. My husband, who is a normally steady and upbeat kind of guy and wakes up smiling, can still become overwhelmed and negative around 3:00 p.m. What I have observed is that he needs a nap. Thankfully, he has the ability to take ten- to twenty-minute power naps. When he wakes up, he is a new man. So if he seems irritable or melancholy, I look at the clock. And I take everything he says with a grain of salt until after his power nap, when he is back to being Mr. Stable and Cheerful. His brain cells just needed some rest. I have my Ph.D. in him as well.

If there is one thing I could tell a person who loves someone who has PTSD, it is this: become more curious than reactive when your loved one is triggered. Notice any patterns you see in her moods and take note of when she seems to be at her best. Is he better able to handle stress when circumstances are calming? Does she need sleep? When did he last eat? Are her hormones out of whack? Does his life/work/play balance need tweaking? Some people with PTSD do best when they are working physically, some when they are outdoors often. Some are best off when they have a lot of unstructured time and "alone time" in their lives. I'm one of those. I need space to be alone with my thoughts—to contemplate meaning in between doing routine tasks. Some PTSD survivors are at their best when they are more socially engaged with a full calendar. Most thrive on a high-nutrition diet, with exercise that suits their personalities and a good night's sleep. Just as all of us do.

As I said before, just as plants grow better under a wide variety of conditions, so too do you and your beloved. Note what conditions help you to be your best self, and also observe what conditions seem to give your partner with PTSD greater feelings of safety, happiness, and calm.

Angst-Free Absorbing Activities

I used to credit the Food Network with helping me overcome PTSD triggers. I got completely caught up in the fun of cooking, the endless variety of personalities and recipes. It was a happy place, the Food Network Channel: an angst-free zone where I could go and get absorbed in ideas for new recipes.

My current angst-free activities are thrift shopping, upcycling, and selling stuff on Etsy and eBay. I am not making any money because I love shopping more than I love selling, but I count it as therapy. I love it—it yields positive feelings and helps me let go of negative thoughts, and it is endlessly interesting and absorbing.

Friends I have known who have PTSD all find relief when they discover an activity that is angst-free and absorbing. For some, it has been learning or improving a sport (golf, soccer, bowling, volleyball, spin classes, etc.); others enjoy a variety of games. Some embark on writing a memoir, some like browsing through Pinterest, and some take up fly fishing or learn to tango. The ideas are as varied as their personalities.

Ask your loved one with PTSD what activities take her to an "angst-free zone"—and if possible, encourage her to enjoy these activities as often as she can, especially after she has been triggered and needs to detach from painful thoughts and move calmly back into the present. At least some of these activities need to be quickly, easily, and readily available. You may love to sky dive, but if you are suddenly triggered into a PTSD episode, then you want to be able to turn to an activity that is handier to engage in right away.

New and Novel Distractions

My therapist once gave me some homework to do something new, something I hadn't done before, about three times a week. "It can be anything at all," he said. "Go to a new restaurant. Try a new food. Attend a new class. Drive a new route. Listen to a new podcast. Try a new sport. Plan ahead for it. Research it. Have fun!"

It seemed an odd request, but there was good science behind it. He knew that I was having trouble with negative, looping thoughts over a current conflict that had triggered some painful memories. At this point, I had done all I could do to mend the personal conflict, and I needed to simply move on. But I was stuck in a thought loop that I couldn't escape! Every time my mind would start to relax, in would come visual pictures of the painful conflict, and my emotions would spiral very quickly into negativity.

What my therapist knew was that the best way to get my brain to unhook from a negative, absorbing, magnetic track was to offer it a new, shiny, interesting, and consuming project. Trying something new takes so much concentration and is so fascinating to our brains that they will even let go of those sticky, negative looping thoughts in order to take on the new task. Our brains love novelty.

This is a great trick for those with PTSD who can't seem to get out of a painful, intrusive mental loop. Try spending a little time with your loved one with PTSD with a pen and a piece of paper, then brainstorm three things you'd each like to try that you've never done before. Two of them could be simple: try a new restaurant, take a drive down an unknown road, or play golf at a new course. Make the third more absorbing, something that will take real planning and research. Maybe it will be a trip to a new city. Or you could decide to take a new class—whether it is to learn how to paint with watercolors or go water-skiing!

Ever had to take away something from a toddler? Experience shows most of us that the easiest way to do this is to offer the toddler something different, something new and novel. So if you want him to give you that heirloom china cup he is holding, be ready to exchange it for a sippy cup full of his favorite juice. Our brains in some ways still function like they did when we were toddlers. To get them to let go of an all-consuming thought loop, we have to offer them something new, exciting, and compelling to ponder and do instead.

Pets

> There are two means of refuge from the miseries of life: music and cats.

> Albert Schweitzer

I have had a mostly wonderful life. Great parents. Good childhood. I have four adult children, three of whom are college graduates with great jobs and spouses and kids, and they've all given me mostly joy most of their lives. I have been married to an amazing man for the last twelve years. But I had a very long, painful, traumatizing marriage, and I also cope with another long-term, chronic, chaotic situation that has not gone away. My eldest son, in his late thirties now, has struggled with addictions for more than twenty years. In the last few years, he has overdosed and almost died three times and has been homeless for most of these years. Like every caring mother, I have turned over every rock I could to try to help him. But he is an adult, and I finally accepted that I cannot save him; I cannot force him to change. I can only love him and pray. It is, needless to say, a huge challenge to maintain mental peace in one of the most chronically sad and frightening situations a parent can face. Letting go and letting God have my eldest boy has been one of the longest and most painful journeys of my life.

About two years ago, my eldest went missing for a very long time. His pattern was to call and check in with me, to let me know he was alive, at least every two or three weeks. As the weeks passed, and then months, with no word, I became a Detective Mom trying to find him, and I grew more and more panicked. On his birthday, my heart was in so much pain—the not knowing, not hearing, thinking the worst. I was driving down an unfamiliar road, praying for him, when I saw a sign for an animal shelter. To this day, I don't know why I did it, but I turned my car around, drove into the parking lot, and walked up to the clerk and asked, "Do you have a kitten for adoption?"

They did. She was a little black-and-white tuxedo kitten with a Marilyn Monroe black "beauty mark" on her face. I took her home, surprising my husband, and we named her Sweet Pea. Her favorite places to snuggle were up around my neck or on my chest. Once settled and comfortable, she would purr and purr. It wasn't long before I noticed that when Sweet Pea was purring, my body would completely relax. I was at peace. I was in the moment. I would often fall asleep.

A few weeks later, while on a trip away from home, I could not seem to relax—worry overwhelmed me. I found a YouTube video of the sound of a purring cat and played it next to my ear, and soon I was more at peace and fell asleep. Later I read that a cat's purr is literally healing: it is the same frequency as the ultrasound machines that physical therapists use to speed healing to muscle and bone.

Eventually, my son surfaced and called after two months. He was not even aware that this much time had passed. But his pattern of disappearing and resurfacing, along with intermittent stints in jail and other kinds of crises, continued. Yet incredibly, I was coping better. This little cat was exactly what the doctor would have ordered for my frazzled nerves.

Six months later, we adopted another kitten, an energetic and affectionate male who we named Rocco. It took a couple of weeks, but Sweet Pea and Rocco became inseparable friends and cuddle buddies. They make us laugh several times a day with their antics and playfulness. When my mind drifts to worry, they pull me back into the simple joy of the present moment. They both love to be held and have fabulous purrs, so now anytime I sit or lie down to relax, it is almost always in the company of at least one cat. To hold a warm, soft animal is a little like forced meditation. Their breathing, their sweetness, their delight in being petted all combine to bring me into the moment and calm my own breathing. They also sense when I am sad, and if I cry, they will put their paws on the trail of tears down my face. They demand so little: I don't have to talk; I don't have to perform. All I have to do is *be*, and they are more than content to just *be* with me.

I could have named Sweet Pea and Rocco "Prozac and Xanax" because they have had such a miraculous effect in helping me with anxiety-producing PTSD symptoms and the chronic challenges of loving an addict. As Charles Dickens said, "What greater gift than the love of a cat?"

I have a friend who lost her young husband, who died quite suddenly and surprisingly in the night. He was the love of her life. She was in shock, in grief, and completely undone, as anyone in that situation would be. In her case, the grief turned into nearly crippling anxiety. But then she got a little white emotional support dog trained to help people with PTSD. With Arthur by her side, my friend was able to attend church; go to work, coffee shops, and restaurants; and have a social life again. Arthur is that warm body beside her that helps her sleep. He brought love and joy back to her days in ways that only an innocent animal can do.

The stories of dogs trained to help calm their owners who suffer from PTSD are incredible. In fact, where drugs and therapy sometimes fail, a loving pet can bring a wounded soldier (of war or of life) back to joy. But in truth, any pet that loves you, calms you, delights you, and needs you can be as curative as medication or therapy without any side effects—other than having to feed them and clean up after them. Whether it is a cat or a dog, a hamster or a horse, I am personally very sold on the idea of owning pets for calming PTSD and for all the joy and love they bring to our lives.

> Dogs have given us their absolute all. We are the center of their universe, we are the focus of their love and faith and trust. They serve us in return for scraps. It is without a doubt the best deal man has ever made.
>
> Roger Caras

Preventative Care

Although you can't avoid every single potential trigger—and you wouldn't want to do so—it is helpful to avoid places and events where triggers are likely to happen. However, at the very least, you should find a way to give your beloved an escape route if he or she should start to feel overwhelmed.

Crowded places with lots of noise are often difficult for those with PTSD. I get anxious with any kind of standing and mingling—such as a cocktail party or even standing in a foyer before church or a cultural event. I love people, but I prefer they all sit down, and I prefer to be with them one or two at a time. My husband knows now that these situations are fraught with potential for me to feel triggered or to melt down. In my former marriage, these sorts of social events, especially parties, were often awkward and traumatizing for me, as my ex-husband would abandon me to flirt and mingle and sometimes even dance with other pretty women. I often felt humiliated or paralyzed, not knowing how to react. Anything I did or said would have, at the time, only provoked more anger and retribution from him.

So if we go to a party, Greg knows I may need to go outside for fresh air or find a quiet room in which to breathe until I feel calm again. He stays near me or checks in on me often. On these occasions, I may take an antianxiety medication ahead of time. As an alternative, we try to socialize in smaller ways whenever possible. If friends ask us to a big party where a lot of people and noise and mingling are expected, we will often decline but offer to meet up for a small dinner instead. Since visiting and mingling in the halls before church sometimes make me feel dizzy and anxious, I either wait quietly outside on a bench (if the weather is pretty) or go to an empty classroom and pray and breathe slowly while my husband (Mr. Social) visits to his heart's content. When I hear the music begin, I go into church and enjoy the service. In other words, as a couple, we have found compromises that accommodate both my husband's need for socializing and my need for feeling safe.

Much of this is common sense and simply involves thinking ahead and preparing. If you are married to a soldier who is triggered by loud noises, you probably don't want to go to monster truck races. If he is triggered by crowds, you will want to be accommodating when possible and avoid them or give him a way to escape them.

My husband has learned what movies, news reports, and TV shows may trigger me, and I have learned his triggers to old pain as well. We watch shows that we can enjoy together, and we give each other our blessing to attend movies alone if we worry it may trigger the other in some negative way. Or I may go upstairs to watch an intense psychological family drama on TV while he watches some action/adventure/drama downstairs. He is triggered by family conflict on the screen; I am triggered by any kind of physical violence.

We show basic caring and courtesy for each other's areas of struggle by avoiding trigger-producing situations when we can, planning ahead for what to do if one of us is triggered, and allowing the other the freedom to enjoy an activity alone. With kindness and creativity, you can design a life with less stress for yourself and your loved one with PTSD.

Be Patient with the Process

As long as your loved one is doing all she can to heal, you will help her best through encouragement. Note any positive improvement. Perhaps he got triggered and had a meltdown or withdrew in response to it. But if you noticed that he also rebounded faster, tell him that! If you notice that the intensity of her episodes is lessening, tell her that you have noticed this and are encouraged.

The truth is, people who have experienced trauma may find the journey to wholeness and health a much longer one than they'd hoped for. Progress, not perfection, is key. If he or she recovers quickly, hooray! But I'd prefer that you be prepared for long, slow improvement over years rather than tell you that your loved one can be instantly cured.

Members of Al-Anon, a support group for those who love alcoholics, use the "three Cs" to remind them of their human limitations: "You didn't cause it, you can't cure it, and you can't control it." This ideology applies to how you should approach your loved one with PTSD as well. You cannot cure her PTSD, despite how much you may wish you could. But although you didn't cause the PTSD and you can't control your loved one's thoughts or actions, there is something you can do: you can be "with them" through his own healing journey. Simply put, you can be an encouraging, supportive friend and fellow pilgrim.

Let us not underestimate how hard it is to be compassionate. Compassion is hard because it requires the inner disposition to go with others to the place where they are weak, vulnerable, lonely, and broken. But this is not our spontaneous response to suffering. What we desire most is to do away with suffering by fleeing from it or finding a quick cure for it.

Henri J. M. Nouwen

Ten Tips for Understanding Someone with PTSD

#1—Knowledge is power. Understanding the process of a triggering event, the psychic reaction to trauma, the warning signs and symptoms of PTSD, and available treatment options for PTSD allows you to help recognize, support, and guide your loved one with PTSD toward diagnosis, treatment, and healing.

We need you to be clearheaded, pulled together, and informed.

#2—Trauma changes us. After trauma, your loved one will want to believe—as will you—that life can return to the way it was. This is not how it works. Trauma leaves a huge and indelible impact on the soul. It is not possible to endure trauma and not experience a psychic shift.

Expect us to be changed. Accept our need to evolve. Support us on this journey.

#3—PTSD hijacks our identity. One of the largest problems with PTSD is that it takes over sufferers' views of themselves. They no longer see clearly. They no longer see the world as they experienced it before trauma. Now every moment is dangerous, unpredictable, and threatening.

Gently remind us and offer opportunities to engage in an identity outside of trauma and PTSD.

#4—We are no longer grounded in our true selves. In light of trauma, your loved one's real self retreats and a coping self emerges to keep him or her safe.

Believe in us; our true selves still exist, even if they are momentarily buried.

#5—We cannot help how we behave. Since those with PTSD are operating on a sort of autopilot, they are not always in control. PTSD is an exaggerated state of survival mode. They experience emotions that frighten and over-whelm them. They act out accordingly in defense of those feelings they cannot control.

Be patient with us; we often cannot stop the anger, tears, or other disruptive behaviors that are so difficult for you to endure.

#6—We cannot be logical. Since your loved one with PTSD's perspective is driven by fear, he or she doesn't always think straight or accept the advice of others.

Keep reaching out, even when your words don't seem to reach us. You never know when we will think of some-thing you said and find that it comforts, guides, soothes, or inspires us.

#7—We cannot just "get over it." From the outside, it's easy to imagine that a certain amount of time passes, memories fade, and trauma gets relegated to the history of a life. Unfortunately, for people with PTSD, nothing fades. Their bodies will not let them forget. Because of surging chemicals that reinforce every memory, they cannot walk away from the past any more than you can walk away from them.

Honor our struggle to make peace with events. Do not rush us. Trying to speed our recovery will only make us cling to it more.

#8—We're not in denial. We're coping! It takes a tremendous effort to live with PTSD. Even if your loved one doesn't admit it, he or she knows there's something wrong. When he denies there's a problem, that's really code for "I'm doing the best I can." Taking the actions you suggest would require too much energy, dividing focus from what is holding her together. Sometimes, simply getting up and continuing her daily routine is the biggest step toward recovery she makes.

Alleviate our stress by giving us a safe space in which we can find support.

#9—We do not hate you. Contrary to the ways people with PTSD might behave when you intervene, somewhere inside, they do know that you are not the source of the problem. Unfortunately, in the moment, they may use your face as PTSD's image. Since they cannot directly address their PTSD issues, sometimes it's easier to address you.

Continue to approach us. We need you to!

#10—Your presence matters. PTSD creates a great sense of isolation. In your loved one's post-traumatic state, it makes a difference to know that there are people who will stand by her. It matters that, although he lashes out, doesn't respond, and is not himself, you are still there, no matter what.

Don't give up; we're doing our best.[10]

---

10   See the website by Michele Rosenthal, "Heal My PTSD," at www.healmyptsd .com.

CHAPTER FOUR

Compassionate Self-Care

I've talked about ways to compassionately companion your loved one with PTSD, but how can you stay happy, healthy, and balanced as well? How do you show up, as Christ would, to offer unconditional love and compassion while accepting that you are also human, with human limitations and needs?

I like the metaphor of a pitcher of water. When I practice self-care and do the things that fill me up, it is like taking the empty vessel of myself to receive water from a well. Only then do I have enough life-giving nourishment to pour out into others. If I find myself pouring out a *lot* of emotional water to someone who is extraneedy or if I'm pouring small amounts of myself into multiple ongoing needs, then I have to make more frequent trips to the well.

The more I pour out, the more I need from that well to fill me up. Jesus talked about Himself as being a well of living water, a well "that never runs dry." But that is because He is the divine Son of God. Human beings, on the other hand, are finite and limited. Thankfully, because Jesus's well is always full, we can go to Him for refillings as often as we need them—even if that means we just take five minutes to breathe and pray and center our souls.

Pause a moment to take in this truth: *The more you care for others, the more you* must *care for yourself, as often as you can, in big and small ways. If you don't, you will burn out, and everybody loses.*

Let's face it, when someone you love has PTSD, it can take a heavy toll on you, both physically and emotionally. If she gets frustrated or angry easily, you may feel like you are walking on eggshells anytime you're around her. And if something you say or do triggers a painful memory, then you may feel personally blamed and emotionally assaulted for something you didn't do. If he is shutting down or closing you out, you may feel rejection and helplessness. Your feelings go from hurt to helpless to numb. People with severe PTSD might also face job loss or substance abuse, which further complicate life.

Besides educating yourself about PTSD (which is why you are reading this book) and trying not to take your loved one's moods personally, the most important thing you can do for him or her is to manage your own stress. The more calm, relaxed, and focused you are, the happier you will be—and your happiness is just as important as your partner's. Also, you'll be able to think clearly and better help your loved one when he or she is triggered.

Know Your Limits

The time to express "I need a break" is before you actually blow up from the stress at hand. Communicating calmly with someone who is having a PTSD meltdown is no easy skill. If a part of your body starts to constrict (your neck, your head, your stomach), your breathing feels shallow, or you feel suddenly flooded with emotion, you will need to call for a break in communication while you gather yourself. It's best to have a phrase that you or your mate can use when you start to feel overwhelmed so you can avoid blowing up and saying damaging things you can't take back.

I have found that simply saying, "I love you, and I'm sorry, but I'm starting to feel overwhelmed and need a little break," works very well, especially if you offer a follow-up time. You could try saying, "Can we try this again in an hour?" or "Could we sleep on this and talk in the morning?" Alternately, if you don't know what to say, buy some time by saying, "Excuse me, I need to use the restroom," and head there to do some breathing exercises. Saying, "Hey, I need to get a little fresh air" or "Let me grab a drink of water" can also buy you a few moments to breathe and clear your head. If you can move a conversation outside, especially if you have rockers or a porch swing—or if you can have a "walk and talk"—it will help you both stay calm.

I know a couple—let's call them Jason and Nora. Jason has PTSD related to a father who never verbally affirmed him. His dad was sometimes abusive, but he was mostly emotionally absent and always negative and impossible to please. Jason was a sensitive boy, and he bears the wounds of never living up to his dad's expectations. He is a hard worker and proud of his work, but one of his triggers is when a customer expresses any disappointment. He tends to handle the customer well, but once he hangs up the phone, he is caught in another world in his head, one where he is trying in vain to prove his worth to his invisible, judgmental father and coming out frustrated, hurt, and angry. Emotions of old rejection flow through his mind and body like a toxic river. Poor Nora would often get caught in the crosshairs of this experience, absorbing Jason's verbalized anger and bad mood and watching his tendency to drink too much after such a PTSD episode. For a long time, she tried to appease and calm Jason, but then she realized that his moods were contagious (she found herself feeling cranky) and getting out of control.

One day, it dawned on her that whenever they went camping or spent a weekend out in nature, Jason could handle customer complaints or phone calls about work problems much better. She told him that next time he got triggered by a grumpy employee, she would only be his sounding board if they first took a walk in fresh air. Then, once they were both feeling calmer, they'd talk. Since Jason and Nora lived in the country, this was an easy solution: nature's bounty was right at their front door.

"By the time we had walked a mile," Nora said, "Jason was calmed by the exercise and the beauty around us—the green pine trees, the shimmering ponds, the birds singing. We'd usually take our bird dog, Bo, out for a walk with us, and Bo always makes Jason smile with his frisky, happy-to-be-outside ways. I too was reaping the benefits of being out in nature and doing something good for my body. On the mile walk back home, Jason and I could usually have a peaceful, productive talk. I'm able to encourage him about what a hard worker he is and how talented he is. And he usually thanks me for caring and listening and understanding. Walking while talking has probably saved our marriage!"

Create Kind Boundaries

Many people misuse the concept of "boundaries in relationships." Good boundaries are not walls to keep people out; they are comfort zones to keep you feeling safe, calm, and secure while you engage with others. Think about your interactions with your loved one who has PTSD. Are you getting your own needs for tranquility and safety met when you talk with him or her?

If triggered, your loved one can get irrational and angry. If you know this, then at a time when things are calm, say, "I know you've been through a lot. You can say anything you need to say, vent as you wish—as long as you do not get disrespectful or verbally abusive to me." Or if you hear his or her voice rising in agitation while you are talking, say, "I need you to keep your voice at a calm and quiet tone. If you can't do that right now, I understand. Let's take a break, and then you can text me when you feel that you are able to be calm and focused again."

Keep Your Well Full with Happy Rituals

To be able to pour love and grace into others, you must have a full well. Everyone "fills their well" differently. I've discovered that to refill my soul, mind, and body, I really require slow mornings without the need to talk very much. Mornings are "me time" while I wake to the world and get oriented to the day. As a writer, I'm often blessed to be able to design my days in a way that allows me to "fill up" before giving out to others who need me. For some people, this may mean spending time in prayer or meditation, reading an uplifting devotional or scriptures, doing a bit of exercise, or sitting outside in the sun. These personal daily rituals of grace help steady us and fill us before we give to, minister for, or serve others.

I don't know if this is because of PTSD or my personality type, but I operate best when I get at least an equal amount of solitude for every hour of socializing. And I get very easily "peopled-out" unless I have frequent breaks. As much as I love to be hospitable, the times Greg and I have allowed people to live with us have proven to be some of the most emotionally draining of my life. Even if the guests are wonderful, having to be "up" and socializing so often drains me quickly. During the holidays, if I have a lot of family in our home for a long time, I create "downtime" in the schedule for everyone every day. This is the time we can use to retreat to our rooms for a nap, watch mindless TV, read, or do whatever fills our wells.

My husband and I often take a short nap during the day, which we can do because he has flexible work hours. We honor each other's need for rest. If I come home from grocery shopping and see that our bedroom door is closed, that is my signal that Greg is taking a power nap. I am as quiet as can be while he rests, and he does the same for me.

Whether or not you are a napper, setting aside some time in your day—even ten or twenty minutes—to do whatever calms and fills your emotional tank is good preventative mind-and-body care. I have friends who love going for a walk or a run (with an iPhone so they can listen to music); another friend swears that her morning yoga class keeps her sane and calm. Others may enjoy a daily trip to the coffee shop to read or journal alone or meet up with a nurturing friend. I remember my very social in-laws, in their retirement years, used to meet up for "pie and coffee" at the local diner with close friends almost every day. This little ritual was a joy to them. If you love and interact with someone who has PTSD, your need for this kind of built-in daily self-care ritual will be an emotional lifesaver. Whatever it takes to carve out some "me time" and keep it sacred—do it. You really can't afford not to.

My husband and I will also encourage each other to take "Greg Days" or "Becky Days." If Greg sees that I am particularly stressed or overwhelmed, he will ask, "Do you need a Becky Day?" On a Becky Day, I am free to do anything and everything I want to do (within reason) at any given minute, all day long, even through dinnertime. So I don't cook or clean or answer the phone. I do anything that sounds delightful—browse a bookstore, treat myself to lunch, take a guilt-free nap, or wander through thrift stores. When Greg needs to disconnect and refuel, he will spend a half day at the movies seeing all those action flicks that I don't particularly love. Or he may go golfing or wander through a store like Best Buy to see all the latest electronic gadgets. We are empty nesters with flexible jobs, so this is much easier for us than for some. But even when I had four children, I would exchange babysitting with another mom or use a church-based (and gloriously affordable) Mother's Day Out once a week to do something that filled my heart with joy. Often this would be having a kid-free lunch out with another mom whose kids were at the same Mother's Day Out!

Get creative with your calendar and see what you can do to arrange regular "me times" into your schedules. Replenish your soul so you can be fully present for others without exhaustion or resentment.

Seek Support of Your Own

Seek out help and support. If your spouse was in the military, there are many resources to help you get support, both online and often in groups that meet face-to-face. Some people with PTSD complicate the issue by turning to substance abuse. If this is your case, you will want to go to your nearest Al-Anon meeting—or at the very least (if meetings aren't your "thing"), read as much of their literature as you can. If your loved one becomes physically violent at any time, the situation is now more than you can possibly deal with alone. Violence tends to escalate. Your spouse will need mentors and possibly good medication to help him or her have more self-control and manage anger. Anger management classes tend to work great … until the person gets truly angry—and then all those lessons fly out the window. Often this has a biological cause. For many people with ADD, ADHD, or brain trauma or other injuries, their prefrontal cortex stops getting blood flow when their emotions are engaged. They literally lose their ability to think clearly, act thoughtfully, and manage impulses wisely. In these cases, medication that lowers their emotional reactivity will be not only helpful for them but life-saving for others.

Final Word

To have a fully functioning, mature relationship, you have to be compassionate to others and compassionate to yourself in a balance that supports your well-being. Give yourself permission to take compassionate, tender care of yourself. Create boundaries that allow time for you to rest and replenish your body and soul. Be kind to yourself, and you will be able to show real kindness to others. Nourish your body with good food, sunshine, fresh air, uplifting music or talks, naps, and fun. You will not only feel better equipped to be a compassionate companion to your loved one, but you will also show her what good self-care looks like and how to prioritize it in her own life.

CHAPTER FIVE

Withdrawing versus Connection

THE HEALING BALANCE

Many men and women return from war profoundly changed—so much so that their families may say, "His body is home, but the person we knew is gone." Or they may get glimpses of the old person they knew and loved but never know when she will suddenly change personalities. Typically, men with PTSD are more withdrawn. But women with PTSD may also withdraw during trauma and its aftershocks. There is a reason for this withdrawal that often has nothing to do with not wanting to connect with others: it is the brain's automatic way of conserving energy when under stress, in much the same way that a wounded animal will go off into the woods to be quiet, still, and alone. It's the nervous system's way of self-healing after being wounded.

Having said this, I realize that it is a real dilemma: How can you honor the time and space that people with PTSD need to heal while also playing a supportive role in helping them "come out of their shell" when it becomes obvious that withdrawing (or "cocooning") is no longer serving them?

When Solitude Is Healing

Recently, I found myself feeling like a deer in headlights. I was completely overwhelmed. I felt some numbness and depression creeping in. My thoughts were jumbled, and I couldn't focus enough to read or write or make a list and complete it. I've felt this way before and recognize that these are not symptoms to be taken lightly. I knew from experience that I needed to address these symptoms with compassionate action because they often signal, for me, that a PTSD meltdown could happen. As I contemplated why I was feeling on the brink of a meltdown, I realized that two young men in my family (my eldest adult son and a nephew) had almost died, and each spent about a month recovering in our home. Though each event happened twelve months apart, the second event (involving my nephew) triggered the trauma I went through when my eldest son almost died a year earlier. I was under the pressure of a big book project, one that required extensive research and footnoting. I had organized, cooked for, and hosted a grand sixtieth birthday party for Greg—complete with lots of overnight company all summer—along with caring, part time, for a young grandson. What had I been missing that year? A single week of pure relaxation. And at that time, at that moment, what I felt I needed most (after a long season of "peopleing" and serving) was some major downtime, along with some solitude.

Thankfully, my kind husband trusts me to tell him what I need to keep from spiraling down, and he had also recognized that it was time for me to do some intensive self-care. I discovered we had a time-share available for a week in Arizona. I found bargain airfare and packed my bags, including one bag full of food to hold me over for the week. Once at the condo, my "schedule" looked like this:

Wake up slowly

Drink iced coffee out on the porch as the sun slowly warms my face

Go to the pool and swim a few laps. Let the sun slowly warm my body

Breathe in, breathe out

Fix a light lunch, take a nap

Read a little, maybe watch a little TV

Eat a light supper

Go sit in the hot tub with a relaxing beverage and look at the moon and stars

Check in with Facebook and talk to my husband

Sleep deeply

I did this for five days. I did not talk to another human soul, except my husband. I withdrew from life for internal repairs for a specific amount of time with a specific purpose: to rest—body, mind, and soul. If anyone observed me, they could only conclude, "Wow, she is really good at doing nothing." And I would have had to agree.

Anne Lamott once observed, "Everything works better when it is unplugged for a bit. Including me."[11] The Bible records that even Jesus "withdrew" from the crowds regularly to go to a mountain and pray. On day six of my personal getaway, I invited a local

---

friend to come to the condo for a day and enjoyed her companionship. By day seven, I was really missing Greg, my family, my cats, and my everyday life. I found that with my head clear, I could write creatively again. In most ways, I felt like a new woman. And all I did was withdraw for a few days to allow my mind and body to repair themselves.

What made my time away so healing was knowing that my husband understood my need to be alone and encouraged me every day by phone to simply relax and enjoy myself. Metaphorically, I felt as though he were waiting and praying for me right outside the door, ready to welcome me back into his arms when I felt more like myself again. I never felt abandoned by him, and he didn't feel abandoned either; he didn't put a single guilt trip on me. In fact, it was like a honeymoon when we saw each other after a week apart.

All that is to say that solitude and withdrawing for a specific amount of time for a specific reason can be very healing. However, no one can truly heal from trauma in a perpetual vacuum.

Being Together in Healing Ways

I talked with my beloved sister last night, and what she shared with me reminded me of how much we all need the company of others to mend our stressed-out souls.

Rachel and her family have survived a decade of chronic financial stress after her husband lost a very good job and was unable to find work that paid a livable salary. She calls it her "riches to rags" story because they moved from a beautiful newer home

www.today.com/popculture/author-anne-lamott-shares-life-wisdom-viral
-facebook-post-t13881.

to an older rental house in a lower-income part of town. She has kept her sense of humor about it all, but there were tears in her eyes as we spoke. She has been through many years of nonstop struggle. She is so tired, working as hard as she possibly can with the best attitude she can muster to help put food on the table— and then their car dies. The repair bill is a month's salary. There is no margin for this. Her husband is also working hard, but for now, there is not enough money at the end of each month to cover basic bills—much less extras for their kids or an emergency fund—and that pains her.

I asked my sister, "What helps you deal with ongoing stress from the traumas in your life?"

She answered, "It mostly helps to not feel alone in this."

My sister's face lit up as she told me about a friend of hers who showed up at the school where she works and brought a beautiful array of fancy deli foods so they could enjoy an impromptu gourmet picnic in the car. Rachel said, "Even though my life had not changed, even though the ongoing trauma of financial struggle was still there, I felt like I was walking on air after that lunch. I felt so grateful and blessed to have a friend who knows me well and refuses to leave my side. She can't fix it, but she can show up, bring lunch, and make me laugh. What is even more poignant is that I have had to turn down other invitations she extended to me because my time is so limited and our budget for 'fun' is nonexistent right now. But this friend is tenacious. She is in this with me. And she found a way to show her concern in a way that I could receive it. I am not alone in this mess. Right now, that is all I need to keep going."

When people go through a dramatic, horrifying, or long and chronic trauma, they can begin to feel like aliens in their own lives. There's much to be said for friends and family who will love them steadily and persistently, place few demands on them, and treat them as "normal" (laugh, talk about daily stuff) but are also tender and compassionate. They need people who aren't appalled or shocked by their "drama" or their history and treat "what happened" as a part of their lives, without it defining who they are today. Good companions lean in instead of away when their loved ones go through a rough time. When journeying out of trauma, people need to be surrounded by those who are unafraid of their pain, their tears, their sorrows, their pasts.

So sometimes people (including you and your loved one with PTSD) need solitude to mend and tend to their souls. And sometimes, we need the company of compassionate friends and family. As long as there is some rhythm and balance to solitude versus social times, your loved one with PTSD is probably doing just fine. A good way to start a conversation is to ask each other, "How much social time versus solitude do you think helps you feel happiest and most balanced?" Don't be surprised if you have different answers. My husband is a social creature and loves a party. I, on the other hand, am drained by too much social interaction. He likes his life to be about 70 percent social and 30 percent solitude or quiet evenings at home with me. I prefer the exact opposite!

What to do? You communicate. You compromise. You figure out a win-win.

Balance between Solitude and Connection

At times, people with PTSD can be very hard to read. You may have no clue what to do with your loved one with PTSD; do you need to give him more space, or do you need to press in and encourage connection? Sometimes people can give conflicting messages, and it feels like they are saying, "Come closer; go away!"—two opposing messages at once. As someone with PTSD, I can tell you that this is often because we really don't know exactly what we want and need when our emotions have overtaken the thinking/processing part of our brains. Also, what we need can shift from hour to hour. I may need a good hard cry one hour, and the next, I'm feeling much better and ready to connect or work. My husband has learned to ask the simple question, "What do you need right now? How can I help?" And I have learned to pause, reflect, come up with an answer, and tell him—even if that answer is, "I don't quite know yet. But you could hold me until I figure it out."

Our relationships can survive almost anything if our truest feelings are communicated with kindness. If you feel confused, then ask your loved one questions until you understand what she needs and wants. Be persistent. And let her know that although you are happy to give her grace and space, you have some needs too—for communication, for clarity, for caring, for intimacy. You need to be a priority in his life, just as he is in yours. Ask him to do his best to tell you how he feels and exactly what he needs and then do the same with him.

One partner may feel abandoned if the other turns inward and isolates too much. My advice is to try to talk it out lovingly and come to a compromise and understanding—to find a healthy balance between solitude and human connection—one that meets both of your needs. If that doesn't work, seek a therapist who can help you find a balance that allows space to heal *and* enjoy relational growth and intimacy.

Recently, my husband and I talked about our needs for alone time and togetherness and created a schedule that works for both of us. Before our talk, he would go to the office and then come home at different times every day, according to his whim, which made it impossible for me to plan my day, and I felt like I could be interrupted at any point. It was driving me crazy. One thing a person with PTSD needs is a life without a lot of surprises—a schedule to depend on. We need routines that nourish us and allow us margin to reflect and repair between busy times, work, and social interaction. So Greg and I put both of our wants and needs on the table and worked out a schedule that gave both of us a bit more structure. And on Sunday nights, we discuss our schedules again and reflect to make sure it allows for a good balance of solitude, couplehood, and socializing that works for both of us.

Walking Each Other Home

When you do get to spend time with your loved one, what can you say or do that will help her enjoy spending time with you? I have said this before, but it is worth repeating: being a companion as someone journeys through any particular valley (PTSD, grief, or loss) is quite different from being a fixer, savior, teacher, mentor, or therapist. You don't have to know all the answers. You just need to be a safe place for your loved one to be with and turn to when she needs you. Simply being a calm, empathetic presence is healing in and of itself.

And it is also important, as I just discussed, that you *let your loved one do the same for you.* You may not have PTSD, but as a human being, you have other struggles and difficult days. There should be some mutual sharing of struggles and giving of empathy. Don't pretend that you have it all together. Be open with your challenges and hurts, as this will help your loved one feel needed and helpful as well. He doesn't always want to be "the one with the problem" or feel like he is "the family issue."

A pastor friend of mine once described life in this way: "We're all going through this muddy river—filled with debris—and sometimes, we feel like we are about to drown. So perhaps a friend drifts by on a log and pulls us up to join him. Down the river a bit, he may fall off, and we'll help him out of the muddy river and onto the log, and on it goes until heaven." We all laughed when he said this, but most of us in the congregation related to the picture. Or, as Anne Lamott says, "We're all just walking each other home."[12]

I also want to mention that when your loved one with PTSD is ready to be social, it is important for her to be with people who support her healing journey. The best kinds of friends for people with PTSD are those who understand the basics of how trauma affects the brain. They are patient with the process; nonjudging, calm, and relaxed; and generally optimistic and kindhearted. They are, as Henri J. M. Nouwen said, people who can "share our pain

---

12   Anne Lamott, *Stitches* (New York: Riverhead Books, 2013), 6, loosely quoting Ram Dass.

and touch our wounds"[13] but do not feel compelled to give lots of advice. They are comfortable with "not knowing, not curing" and identifying (showing empathy) in compassionate solidarity, human being to human being.

It may seem odd to include a whole chapter on the balance between socializing and solitude and talking about your individual needs for each. But it is an issue that I have observed again and again when one of the people in a relationship has PTSD. For those with PTSD, the world of socializing can be fraught with potential triggers, and in my observation, those with PTSD tend to prefer being alone or being at home with just the family or with a close friend or two. I was chatting with a young veteran who served in Afghanistan about PTSD recently. We were at a small Starbucks, and it suddenly got very crowded. He asked if we could go outside to finish our conversation. He explained why later: "When in combat, you always want to be aware of your surroundings and be able to easily escape. When I'm in a closed space with lots of people, I start to feel panicky. I've seen too many buildings bombed, I guess. I need to be able to see the door and exit quickly."

Just be aware that if your loved one with PTSD prefers a less active social calendar and quieter spaces or uncrowded places, there is likely an underlying reason for this. Show mutual compassion and caring, talk it through, and you'll find your way to a balance that honors both of your needs.

---

13   Henri J. M. Nouwen, *Out of Solitude* (Notre Dame, IN: Ave Maria Press, 2004), 38.

CHAPTER SIX

Trauma as Delayed Grief

Trauma, grief, and PTSD are often overlapping experiences. Dr. Alan Wolfelt examines this overlap in his thought-provoking book *Reframing PTSD as Traumatic Grief*. In short, he believes that PTSD is another term for "carried grief"—a type of "leftover grief" that we carry with us until it is safe enough to stop and "unpack" it in the company of a compassionate friend or therapist. Traumatic experiences can be so overwhelming for the psyche that some of the pain gets stored away until we are better able to process it and grieve. Dr. Wolfelt calls this "catch-up mourning."

My dear friend Melissa lost her son in a tragic accident. She grieved deeply for a very long time, as any loving mother would. But then she was able to put her grief into a season of honoring her son through productive action. Melissa began to teach, she got her bachelor's degree, and then she went on for her master's degree. She and her husband became new grandparents, and they also built their dream house together. Then more than a decade later—*whoomf*!—some old unmourned grief fell off the shelf into Melissa's lap, and there she was, coping with crying and waves of sorrow and overwhelming emotion, much as she had done right after her son died. What happened? I believe that when she lost her child, Melissa grieved as much as her psyche could allow at the time. And then she had a reprieve as new projects and goals and happy events carried her back into life, sort of like the way diseases go into remission. But with all these new experiences and the passage of time, new aspects of grief sprung up: her son would have loved being an uncle to the two precious nieces he would never meet. She could imagine her son, had he lived beyond age twenty, happily married and bringing his own wife and kids to the newly built dream home, splashing around in the pool and enjoying meals on the patio.

These thoughts brought on fresh feelings of loss that begged to be honored and mourned as well. So she wisely tended to her heart, went back to therapy, and prioritized her well-being as she grieved. A therapist could have diagnosed my friend with PTSD and said that the new events were triggers to old pain. And that may have been true, but "delayed grief" and "catch-up mourning" are perhaps even more accurate terms to describe what Melissa experienced.

If your loved one has PTSD and he is in therapy where he is finally releasing trauma memories in a safe space, there will be some catch-up mourning to be done, and he may come home from therapy looking and feeling worse rather than better for a little while. This is because he is going through grief that may have been delayed. And this experience may involve all the classics steps of grief for him, from shock to denial to bargaining to anger to acceptance. Expect waves of weeping and emotions all over the map. If so, then you may find it easier to comfort your loved one if you think of her as grieving an unmourned loss rather than having a PTSD episode. This way of framing her sorrow may also lead you to ask some deeper and better questions: "What have you lost that is causing so much hurt, my love?" "I can see you are in grief today over something that is causing you pain. Can I hold you? Can I bring you anything?" "How can I be with you that may be of some comfort?"

Healing Doesn't Mean Erasing

Before we get too far into this chapter, I want to emphasize that healing—deep healing—can't be hurried. It doesn't mean that people have to put their whole lives completely on hold while they heal; engaging in life has its own healing power. But I want you to relax and accept the process. Put aside any deadlines you might have had for "healing from trauma." On this side of heaven, we may never completely heal from trauma's effect on us. Nor does God always desire this to happen.

We are wounded healers, and our wounds often allow us to bond more deeply with fellow sufferers in this pilgrimage of life. In Thornton Wilder's *The Angel That Troubled the Waters and Other Plays*, an angel holds back a physician who has a physical impairment from entering healing waters with these words: "Without your wounds, where would your power be? The very angels themselves cannot persuade the wretched and blundering children on earth as can one human being broken in the wheels of living. In Love's service, only the wounded soldiers can serve."[14]

---

14   Thornton Wilder, *The Angel That Troubled the Waters and Other Plays* (New York: Coward-McCann, 1928).

The angel was trying to tell the aching physician that it was his very wounds that made him most qualified to do his job—to help heal the sick—with the kind of compassion ("suffering with") that also heals souls. In other words, as much as you would like to erase all the bad memories in your loved one's past, it may be those very experiences that God will use and transform for good. It's been said that our greatest misery is where our ministry will be. Because of my own trauma, I have been much more effective in comforting others going through crisis or grief or trauma. People know that I've been through a lot of trauma in my life and that I deal with PTSD, and when they see me smiling and hopeful, they are encouraged that they too can live full and happy lives, even with trauma as part of their stories. "In Love's service, only the wounded soldiers can serve."[15]

God is in the business of turning ashes into beauty, personal trauma into a ministry of compassion. Nothing that we have experienced, given to Him, goes to waste.

Wounds Without, Wounds Within

God is a refuge for the broken, not a shelf for the display of the shiny.

Michele Cushatt, *Undone*

Michele Cushatt is the author of *Undone: Making Peace with an Imperfect Life*.[16] She is a dear friend of mine and has survived one of the most painful cancers imaginable. The hellish experiences she

---

15 Wilder, *Angel That Troubled the Waters*.
16 Also see Michele's blog and website at www.michelecushatt.com.

endured and the aftermath of multiple excruciating surgeries left her feeling like a shell of her former self. However, once she made it through the worst of the physical trauma, some people told her that she should be rejoicing. She should be grateful and happy! And she was: she bravely put one foot in front of the other and reentered life as fully and as best she could, but the trauma she endured had changed her. There is no erasing that, no throwing pink paint on this new reality. Where does a woman go to grieve what she lost after "winning" a horrific battle with cancer? Where can she get the time and compassion needed to adjust to the absence of her former, energetic self? The moment she appeared to be outwardly healed, she was pressed back into service as wife/mom/employee/ friend.

In addition to going through the ravages of cancer, my friend has young children with special needs and a career that she needs to attend to if bills are to be paid. It's a *lot*. Michele is doing the best she can, but the truth is, now that the worst of the physical trauma is over, the grief over the many losses this cancer exacted from her is just beginning. She can't simply snap out of it. This is a grief that must be tended to with loving care as best she can, whenever she can.

Though someone with PTSD may look well on the outside after a physical trauma (whether it was caused by violence or from illness, disease, or accident) he may be just beginning the true inner healing. Trauma and its effects won't disappear overnight; and in truth, some parts of PTSD may never completely go away. What you can do is to give your loved one space, time, and permission to go at his own pace in healing. Assure him that as long as he is working on getting better, you have no expectations or deadlines for how long that will take.

If I were talking to someone who had survived a trauma, I would say, "Take the time to heal as much as you can—as much as your mind and body and basic life demands allow. Don't put it off for some other day. The more you put it off, the deeper trauma embeds itself into your psyche. Prioritize your mental healing the same way you would prioritize healing from cancer or major surgery. Don't just roll back into life full-steam ahead. Honor what your body has survived by honoring your emotional wounds and giving yourself what you need to heal."

Also, in the case of disease or illness, emotional well-being is a big factor in healing and staying healthy. That's why caring for emotions has a positive effect on physical health. Use the word *self-compassion* with your loved one, and encourage her to nourish and be very kind and gentle with herself. A lot of anger at others stems from being angry and intolerant of our own selves. By reminding those with PTSD to treat themselves as they would a hurting child, they will eventually be more kind, tender, and patient with everyone.

Writing Trauma into a Life Story

You play the hand you're dealt. You play it without false hope or despair, without comparing other people's hand, or questioning why you've got this hand, you just play it, as best you can, today, and the next day, and the day after that.

Lindsey O'Connor, *The Long Awakening*

After trauma, people face an emotional task that I call "folding past pain into a new story." What does that mean? It means assimilating their painful stories into the larger book of their lives. Those with PTSD are not only recovering from trauma but will eventually be involved in the process of creating a new story and new identity—post-trauma. They cannot go back to an old normal; that door was shut with the arrival of a severe trauma. They may have semisuccessfully buried the trauma from their conscious memories and functioned for a while, but trauma has not disappeared; it is still waiting on the shelf to be dealt with, to be assimilated into new realities. And remember that part of what your loved one is grieving is the "old self" that was altered or destroyed by trauma.

What does this look like, exactly?

Let's go back to the previous example. A loved one may have survived a painful, traumatic battle involving his health, whether it was cancer or an accident or any other life-threatening medical emergency. He lived, and this is truly wonderful. But severe medical trauma exacts a price, even from its survivors, depending on how invasive and long and traumatic the treatment. Radiation and chemo, extensive surgeries, and painful rehabilitation can be traumatizing in and of themselves, but they may also cause permanent changes to the brain and body. So while friends and family may be rejoicing, relieved that the worst of the health crisis is over, the person with the trauma experience may just now be able to cope with what happened. Now that he is safe and going to live, your loved one may experience triggers and night terrors and depression—PTSD in full swing, traumatic grief in full expression. Instead of gratitude and calm, your loved one may be angry or avoidant or weeping in sorrow. He may have physically survived, and the scars may even be healing, but his journey through grief is just beginning. And again, for most who have survived any kind of major life crisis, one of the first things they will grieve is the loss of the self they used to be.

One of my closest friends is Lindsey O'Connor, who suffered a ruptured uterus after she delivered her fifth child, a baby girl, and had to be put into a medically induced coma for several months. Her life was in limbo. The doctors did not know if she would survive or, if she did, whether her brain would function again. Lindsey describes her journey eloquently in her beautifully written memoir *The Long Awakening*. The fact that Lindsey lived and seemed to be her old self was truly a miracle. People were rejoicing and beyond thrilled. But among other losses, Lindsey had missed the first months of her baby girl's life and all the normal bonding with a newborn.

No doubt, she was thankful for the years ahead to be this child's mother—a gift beyond measure. But from Lindsey's perspective, she had just given birth to a newborn, then woke up to a two-month-old baby. It was a shock. She missed nursing her newborn, seeing her baby's first smile, and rocking that soft tiny body over hours of bonding, and these losses were huge to a woman who had spent nine months dreaming of mothering a newborn again. Though nobody else could see much difference, Lindsey also suffered from lack of oxygen to her brain that caused small traumatic brain injuries, and Lindsey noticed—especially in the first year of healing—that her mental processing speed was not what it once was. That was a huge loss to someone who'd always depended on her quick and sharp mind in her job as journalist and writer. Moreover, her lungs had been scarred by a respiratory distress syndrome called ARDS. She did not escape the coma unscathed. She felt disoriented, suffered night terrors, and had many other lingering health issues. If you saw Lindsey today, you would see a beautiful and brilliant woman with a smile that lights up every room and a sharp mind and keen wit. However, she will be the first to tell you that trauma exacted a price from her body and brain and that it has taken time, love, work, and tenderness to create and grow into her new identity—postcoma, post-trauma. A professional author and journalist, it took a full ten years before Lindsey felt ready to write the story of her awakening because it was much more than waking up from a coma—it was waking up to a new reality. It was a new story to fold into her old story that had been suddenly interrupted by major trauma. Until she could mentally, spiritually, and emotionally weave the "life before the coma" into her "life now" in a meaningful way, she was not ready to share what had happened to her in writing. She was still busy figuring that out and also coming to terms with who she was now and who she wanted to be in her future. Why did these things happen to her? Was there meaning in any of it? Where was God in all of this? Moving through these issues took time, support, and understanding.

Again, people don't have to put their lives completely on hold while healing from PTSD and trauma, but we also shouldn't put pressure on them to simply hurry up and get over it. What can you say to someone who is on this long journey? "Take all the time you need. There is no rush for this. Just as a wound heals slowly, layer by layer, so your mind will also heal. And just as you need nutrition, fresh air, rest, and therapy to heal from a physical trauma, you will need all these things to support your healing from the aftereffects, the emotional trauma."

Some people heal from PTSD fairly quickly on their own. This could be because they have genetically less anxious and more resilient brains or because the trauma was a one-time event, was not terribly severe, and was tended to right away with good help and compassion. Some need just a few sessions with a therapist. Some will never get completely over the occasional nightmares or intrusive thoughts or triggers, but these instances will lessen in frequency and duration if these people are working on their overall well-being. Sometimes healing is two steps forward and one step back. Sometimes people deal with a trauma memory as it surfaces—a little bit here, a little bit there—in a variety of ways because to go into it too deeply for too long is more than they can handle.

Can you see how this process is unique to every person? Healing from PTSD, in my opinion, is much more art than science, although there is good brain science behind the art of healing. And from my experience, once someone has a "trauma toolbox" filled with a variety of practical ways to self-soothe and heal, she becomes her own expert at putting together her own program of PTSD healing at her own pace (more on this in the next chapter). You may want to tell your loved one, "I believe that you and your body will tell you exactly what you need to heal from this. Get all the information you can and then trust yourself to sort through it and choose what you feel will be most helpful."

To sum up this section, the task of healing from PTSD is much like the task of grieving: it involves mourning losses and creating a new self that folds the story of your pain/hurt/trauma/loss into your new life in a meaningful and hopeful way. This won't happen overnight; it takes a long time to take off an old identity and create a new one to put on that fits well. The good news is that when the process is done, often with the help of a good counselor who is an expert in PTSD, most people love their new selves much more than the old ones. This new self is more aware of both the fragility and the blessing of life, more real and honest, and more open. Life is less about the image and success and more about the soul and spiritual meaning.

Trauma Recovery Is Tiring

As your loved one does the emotional work of trauma recovery and making meaning from it in his life now, you may notice things getting worse for a bit before they get better. Also, he may look and feel tired.

Why is that?

Newly pregnant women are amazed at how fatigued they are as their bodies channel their limited energy toward creating new life. In some ways, your loved one's brain is doing something similar: it is busy letting go of one "normal" and finding ways to assimilate a new normal. It's tiring brain work, and it may also temporarily deplete happy neurotransmitters like dopamine and serotonin. Your instinct may be to want to minimize your loved one's pain, to brush over it or ignore it, or make him do activities that you believe will make him happier and lift his mood. I get this. I used to think that when someone was depressed, it was my job to cheer her up—to fix her. It's what nurturing people do, right?

I am, by nature, a sanguine Pollyanna, a cockeyed optimist. But during and after severe personal trauma, I got fully acquainted with the dark side of moods, with what depression feels like. There were weeks when I dreaded the sunrise, longing to stay wrapped in the cocoon of my soft, safe bed. Even after I'd make the gargantuan effort of getting up and dressed, I kept glancing at the clock, longing for bedtime and the blessed unconsciousness that came with sleep. My creativity vanished. My brain in a fog, writing became a convoluted and impossible task. And the sleepiness! Who knew grieving could be so exhausting? I could barely fit my life into my newly jam-packed sleeping schedule.

There is a commercial for an antidepressant that says, "Where does depression hurt? Everywhere." As hokey as the commercial may be, it is true. Depression affects the same areas of our brains that process physical pain. I felt it in my gut, as if it had transformed into a giant pretzel made of rock. Some people feel grief in a vice-like squeeze around their chests and fear they may be having a heart attack. I call these "grief spasms." Do not be surprised if during therapy for PTSD, your loved one is extra tired or experiences some physical pain as well.

Both PTSD and Grief Affect Mental Processing

Not only does a highly stressful or agonizing experience make a body feel tired or achy, but it can also make one feel profoundly stupid. The brain borrows neurons once available to make lists, think creatively, and focus on responsibilities to use in the emergency task of coping with a loss, processing painful emotions, and rewiring itself to accept and adjust to new realities, writing the story of the new you, post-trauma. While this is happening, your loved one may have precious little brain power left over for regular tasks and social interactions. Her to-do list may shrink to getting one or two things done per day. He may be more forgetful and only capable of things that require short windows of attention. I can't tell you how much it will mean to your beloved if you acknowledge that healing is exhausting work and don't pressure her to do more than she can do.

Other Symptoms

People with PTSD—just like any person going through normal grief—may lose their appetites for many things they formerly loved: good food, reading, going out with friends. Do not despair; this is temporary. It will all come back once their brains have gone through the process of healing old memories and incorporating trauma into a new normal. Again, just as healing from a major surgery takes time, so healing from a freshly reopened emotional wound takes time.

What can you do to support them as they heal? The next chapter will offer a menu of ideas or a toolbox full of suggestions that have helped many people. Pick one or two that sound good to you and give them a try. By trial and error, you may discover some new ways to be a huge comfort and help to your loved one with PTSD.

CHAPTER SEVEN

The Healing Toolbox

As you have probably noted, healing from trauma is unique to each person's experience, genetics, and brain chemistry. As much as I wish there was a "one-size-fits-all" treatment for PTSD, there will be some trial and error while your loved one figures out what helps him or her the most. Rather than imagining your partner's journey toward healing as some kind of list or prescriptive method, it is better to imagine a mental health toolbox that is filled with a variety of tools that he or she can use at any time, in any situation.

Note Triggers

Scientists are learning that trauma doesn't just affect the brain; instead, it permeates cells all over our bodies. This is why we may be triggered by an event (or smell or sound) that links to a painful memory without ever consciously processing it in our brains. It has become a body memory. During some of my most traumatic experiences, I lived in Texas, where country songs were often playing in the background. Country music, like pickup trucks, permeates the Lone Star State. At the time, I didn't make any conscious connection between painful experiences and the music that played in the background. Interestingly, however, many years later, just a few strains of any country song on the radio can make me feel sad, agitated, and anxious all at once. Greg has learned that if he doesn't want to mess with my happy mood on car trips, it's best to avoid turning the dial anywhere near a country music station.

If you have PTSD, I bet you've discovered something similar: a smell or a song, a scene in a movie, or a tone in someone's voice can trigger feelings from long-ago pain in the very cells of your body. Perhaps your stomach tenses up or your eyes water or your mood drops. And it may take your brain a few minutes to comprehend what's happening on a logical level. This is what body memories are like. The trauma could even be fairly benign. My husband feels nauseous at the sight of green beans or cherries. He worked summers in a green bean cannery and got his fill of them for a lifetime. And once, as a boy, he ate so many cherries from the neighbor's cherry tree that he got violently sick—he hasn't touched a cherry since.

All this to say that your loved one may end up having a PTSD episode of some sort—feeling suddenly frozen or detached or over-whelmed and weepy and shaken—without having any conscious thoughts. He may have no idea why he is suddenly feeling awful. This is where being a bit of a detective comes in handy. When your loved one is able to talk about what happened, try saying, "Let's just think for a minute. What was happening just before you got hit with bad feelings? Did the sun go behind the clouds? Did you smell something? Hear something? See something that could have triggered old pain?" It helps to isolate the cause for two reasons: (1) so the person doesn't feel confused and helpless by her own emotional reaction to what seemed like nothing at all and (2) to help you avoid the trigger next time or to better prepare for it.

Knowing the exact trigger is helpful, but what can you do to help your loved one exit an episode?

Use the Rocking Cure

It's the simplest of soothing, sleep-inducing remedies, something we all naturally do: rocking a baby gently to sleep. Long after we've left childhood, we all can be deeply affected by this relaxing rocking motion. Think of the peaceful glide of a porch swing, sleeping on a boat, or the calming sway of a hammock nap.

Dr. Michael Breus, the "Sleep Doctor"

A variety of trauma specialists from all parts of the world have found that one sure way to help people release trauma, especially when it is held in the body, is to do some form of back and forth swaying movement. Scientists aren't completely sure why this works; they only know that it does. This rocking, rhythmic movement can take many forms in therapy. Eye movement desensitization and reprocessing (EMDR) involves retelling your painful stories in the presence of an EMDR-trained therapist while following the back and forth movement of a therapist's finger or holding a device in each hand that buzzes back and forth. It is one of the classic treatments for PTSD that I will discuss further in the next chapter. Psychiatrists who specialize in helping children with trauma often recommend that parents (or new adoptive parents) rock their kids (even if they are older). Swinging is another comforting, self-soothing activity children can do. There are even special swings made of fabric that fold like a blanket around kids as they swing to add the comfort of cocooning to the comfort of swinging.

Interestingly, one trauma specialist found that he could help groups of civilians who'd been exposed to violence release stored trauma all at once by simply having them stand up and sway or sit and rock back and forth. Once expressionless, after a few minutes of this rocking activity, the civilians' faces came alive again. Some cried, some talked, but all got unstuck from trauma's grip. I am not sure why this works, but I think it all goes back to the way we were soothed as babies when we were swaddled and rocked or bounced or put in a swing. It's the way God wired us to soothe and be soothed both in infancy and beyond.

If you find that you can't sleep because of intrusive negative thoughts, try this: get up and go to another room, then swing your arms back and forth like a gorilla or side to side like a rag doll. It may look and feel silly, but it works beautifully to stop a negative, painful thought loop. Latch onto whatever repetitive movement you enjoy that soothes your brain. I have a porch swing, a hammock, rockers on my back porch, and a living room that has three rocking chairs—I call it the "Rocking Room." Rocking is soothing to people of all ages, but if you love someone with PTSD, you will find that any investment into furniture that sways or rocks pays off in wonderful emotional benefits. Even children who don't have trauma but are simply upset or cranky are responsive to swinging, rocking, or swaying. You can often calm a child in seconds by encouraging him or her to "go outside and swing" or "rock your baby doll" if he or she is feeling stressed or overwhelmed.

When you are in a more neutral and relaxed state, try to spend a few moments in prayer, listen to a comforting piece of music, or read some calming scripture or quotes or inspirational thoughts. Once you've calmed your brain with rhythmic movement, your mind is much more open and receptive to positive truth and healing words. I sometimes wonder if Jesus, the master teacher and healer, spent lots of time on boats and walking with His disciples because the waves of the water and the rhythm of walking allowed their minds to relax as He shared stories of heaven's truth with them and posed questions for them to ponder.

Shake It Off Naturally

Dr. David Berceli, a former monk, has worked with traumatized groups of people all over the world. Through this work, he developed tension- and trauma-releasing exercises (TRE), a sequence of exercises that stimulate trembling in the muscles to let off stored trauma. You can google TRE and PTSD to find out more about books, DVDs, and even YouTube videos that can give more specifics on this method, along with pros and cons.[17]

Engaging Large Muscles

Engaging the large muscles also releases neurotransmitters that calm stress (e.g., doing pull-ups or calf raises). Carrying relatively weighty objects or backpacks or working out with weights can help discharge some of the adrenaline buildup. Even engaging the

---

17   See also the TRE website, "Tension & Trauma Releasing Exercises," TRE
     For All Inc., n.d., https://traumaprevention.com/.

muscles of the jaw can help. Chewing sugar-free gum can calm the brain and body.

Use Cocooning

When infants are overwhelmed or overstimulated, they will often calm if they are swaddled, right? Similarly, your loved one may relax faster after a PTSD episode when wrapped tightly in your arms or a blanket. For example, when I get triggered, I wrap myself up in my heated throw blanket. This tangible thing instantly provides a sense of comfort for me. For those in warmer climates, check into lightweight blankets made of layers of cotton gauze. They are soft as a breeze, not too hot, and feel comforting as a cocoon. When kids are overstimulated, they prefer a nest of sorts, like a small tent or even a closet or corner in which to curl up and calm down. There are tents that fit over single beds now that provide perfect cocooning spots for people of any age.[18]

Use Your Hands in a Repetitive Task

Kelly Lambert, Ph.D., researcher and author of the book *Lifting Depression: A Neuroscientist's Hands-On Approach to Activating Your Brain's Healing Power*, discovered that doing something productive and repetitive with your hands—knitting, stirring, vacuuming, shelling peas, or quilting—engages something she calls the "effort-driven reward loop." So if your loved one with PTSD is out of sorts, think of tasks or hobbies she enjoys that use her hands and steer her that direction. What about playing an instrument, sanding and

---

18   See the website at www.privacypop.com.

painting an old piece of furniture, making pasta from scratch, or coloring an intricate picture in one of those popular coloring books for adults? All these activities are calming and lift the mood.

Breathe

Breathing slowly in and out from the tummy is a helpful way to regulate oxygen and initiate feelings of calm. Remember the Lamaze breathing techniques that help diminish pain in natural childbirth? You can use them to help calm a loved one who is having a panic attack. Another method is to close one nostril with your finger and then breathe in and out. Alternate and do the same with the other nostril. Go back and forth for about a minute.

Seek Water

I've always found calm around the rhythm of water, whether it is doing the backstroke as I float in a pool or watching ocean waves roll in and out. Even fish swimming rhythmically in a fish tank can calm my brain. A hot shower or a hot tub full of bubbles is instantly calming to most of us, children and adults alike. Water sports such as kayaking, canoeing, surfing, waterskiing, or sailing make for great activities to both burn off energy and use the rhythmic calming power of moving water to promote feelings of peace, safety, and release.

Cry Productive Tears

A good cry is a gift. According to Judith Orloff, M.D., "emotional tears have special health benefits. Biochemist and 'tear expert' Dr. William Frey at the Ramsey Medical Center in

Minneapolis discovered that reflex tears are 98% water, whereas emotional tears also contain stress hormones which get excreted from the body through crying. After studying the composition of tears, Dr. Frey found that emotional tears shed these hormones and other toxins which accumulate during stress."[19] Other studies also suggest that crying can stimulate "the production of endorphins, our body's natural pain killers and 'feelgood' hormones."[20]

Remind your loved one that his tears are precious to God and that he may feel better after letting the tears flow. The psalmist tells us that God saves our tears in a bottle. The original term for this bottle was actually a "wine-making flask." God sees every teardrop, saves them like the finest grapes (as your sorrow is precious to Him), then transforms your heartbroken tears into something beautiful, rich, and life giving that will quench another's thirst and bring comfort and joy to many.

> Don't ever discount the wonder of your tears. They can be healing waters and a stream of joy. Sometimes they are the best words the heart can speak.
>
> William Paul Young, *The Shack*

---

19   Judith Orloff, "The Health Benefits of Tears," *Psychology Today, Emotional Freedom* (blog), July 27, 2010, www.psychologytoday.com/blog/emotional -freedom/201007/the-health-benefits-tears. Article adapted from Orloff's book *Emotional Freedom: Liberate Yourself from Negative Emotions and Transform Your Life*.

20   Brynn Taylor, "Sad Things That Are Actually Awesome," *Hot Salad World*, March 3, 2017, www.hotsaladworld.com/news-1/2017/3/3/sad-things-that -are-actually-awesome.

Make a Self-Soothing List

> Do not think that happiness must keep its distance so long as you have so much to pass through. The more you have to pass through, the more you need happiness.
>
> Christian D. Larson, *Just Be Glad*

When your loved one has a hard day, her thoughts can get so kidnapped and overfocused on past pain that she may forget to do even the little things that nourish her mind with tender-loving acts of self-care. It's a good idea, in fact, to help her create a list of things to soothe her troubled soul. Here are a few ideas:

Sit outside in the sun and watch the clouds roll by

Take a hot bubble bath with vanilla or lavender scent

Organize one thing: your purse, a drawer, your jewelry

Go for a walk, a bike ride, or a drive in the country

Meet a friend who is a good listener

Get a massage

Talk to a counselor, wise mentor, spiritual director, trusted pastor, or life coach

Read an uplifting book

Take a guilt-free nap—if it is a pretty day, buy a hammock and enjoy a nature nap. If it is cold outside, use a soft, heated throw or blanket and relax into dreamland

Quilt, knit, or crochet

Browse through Pinterest, watch Food Network shows, try new recipes (Can I boldly recommend my funny mother-daughter food memoir, *We Laugh, We Cry, We Cook?*)

Cuddle or walk a pet

Go hit some golf balls or shoot some baskets

Go to a zoo or aquarium, an art museum, or anywhere fascinating and soothing

Babysit for someone (if babies and/or children lift your spirits)

Read a funny book or watch a comedy show

Play or learn to play a musical instrument

Take a class in something, be it pottery, watercolor painting, or rock climbing

Go on a retreat that interests you

Buy or pick flowers and arrange them

Mow the lawn or vacuum the carpet (repetitive tasks calm the brain)

Play cards or other games

Cook or bake something soothing

Use Centering Prayer

Many authors and musicians produce books and audio recordings that can help your loved one relax through something called centering or healing prayers. I highly recommend two CDs by Nigel Mumford, an Episcopal priest who is driven to help God's children find emotional healing: *Relaxation and Healing Prayer* and *The Essence of Soaking Prayer*. Nigel reads scriptures and prayers in his comforting British accent as soft music plays. It's wonderful for helping one fall asleep feeling loved by God, and it's very good for anyone who is in the hospital or going through chemo. These CDs and others like them can be especially soothing companions, like a portable "healing shepherd." (Nigel, a former British marine, says, "As a former Marine Commando drill instructor, I used to make grown men cry. I still do, but in a different way!"[21])

Have a Health-Centered Focus

Being physically healthy and making nutrition, movement, and playfulness priorities will support both you and your loved one with PTSD. Check out diets that are proven to be especially good for the brain and heart and that reduce inflammation in the body. I have a friend who suffered from depression, PTSD, alcoholism, and brain fog. One day, he read a book about giving up wheat and other foods that often cause allergies or inflammation. Within a month, he was a new person. His cravings for alcohol went away, and he began to feel so much better that he started to exercise. Soon after, he realized that his creativity and ability to focus had returned. His PTSD symptoms and depression went away. His story goes to show that you never know what a change in diet will do to help support healing and recovery.

As I've discussed, movement of any kind can help dislodge trauma from the body and break what can feel like a "trauma trance," wherein your loved one may feel immobilized by an old memory or new trigger.

I am one of those people who do not love the gym or the word *exercise*. I have to bribe myself into any kind of movement or action. On my way to work out, I'll grab a special coffee as an energy-boosting reward. Or I'll go shopping (something I love) but first make myself go up and down the aisles at a good pace to

---

21   See the By His Wounds Christian Ministry home page at www.byhiswounds ministry.org.

get my heart beating. Or I'll listen to a podcast or an audiobook as I walk. Sometimes I'll watch a favorite TV show while I do yoga or floor exercises. I love finding and fixing up old furniture, a task that requires a lot of movement, so doing this feels more like play than work for me. Maybe you will find a project that motivates you to move more. Redecorating an old room, fixing up a man cave or garage, or organizing all the closets in the house could encourage you to get that body off the couch and into gear. For some inspiration, you can check out *The Life-Changing Magic of Tidying Up: The Japanese Art of Decluttering and Organizing* by Marie Kondō (2014) and *Clutter Free: Quick and Easy Steps to Simplifying Your Space* by Kathi Lipp (2015), two great go-to books for motivating you to organize your home. Also, dealing with physical clutter has a ripple effect on helping you also deal with mental clutter. Being in a clean, beautiful space is calming to the mind and supportive of healing efforts.

I also recommend that you look into supplements and alternative medicine. Because people who are born with the genetic predisposition for anxiety are also more susceptible to PTSD, any protocol that helps calm anxiety will also lessen PTSD symptoms. Things like regular massages, acupuncture, biofeedback, oxygen therapy, or a relaxation class may be helpful for you and your loved one as you calm your minds with soothing activities and specialized antianxiety supplements.

I hope this chapter has given you some practical ideas to pack into your loved one's healing toolbox—and don't forget to try some of them on yourself as well when you feel overwhelmed.

CHAPTER EIGHT

Professional Therapies

Though you can be a huge support to your loved one with PTSD, he or she will ultimately need to seek out the best professional help available, especially if PTSD is interfering with his or her happiness or the happiness of others.

There is a wide assortment of techniques, therapies, books, and articles on ways to help people free themselves from the grip that PTSD has on their minds and lives. All the therapies aim to help people with PTSD in the following areas:

- *Self-soothing.* Learn ways to calm their own minds and bodies when they are alone or in a stressful situation.
- *Self-trust.* Learn to hear their own voices within and to trust those voices.
- *Self-compassion.* If PTSD stems from any kind of abuse or neglect, then self-compassion needs to be taught or relearned. Too often, people with PTSD hear the voices of their abusers in their heads when going about their lives. They need a new voice, one of unconditional love and kindness, patience, and support.

- *Self-regulation.* When triggered, people with PTSD often go into shut-down mode or explode. Self-regulation techniques are learned skills that can help redirect the rush of adrenaline by teaching one how to detach and observe the body's responses rather than automatically following them.

- *Communication of needs and desires and limits or boundaries.* Many people who grew up with childhood or relational trauma have trouble recognizing their basic needs for balance and well-being and feel guilty asking for the things they need. Learning to set limits, to say no, and to ask kindly for what they need will prevent blowups and melt-downs from overload.

- *Accurate perception of others.* You may inadvertently trigger your loved one by something you say, and he or she may then overlap the abuser—in that moment—with you. A good therapist can help give your loved one some perspective and the ability to differentiate between normal human flaws, mistakes, and disagreements and abuse.

Though you are not the person who will be going through therapy for PTSD, the more you know about the treatment options available and how they may help your loved one, the better you can understand and support him and perhaps even help him decide on treatments that may be most helpful for his situation. Experts treat trauma in several ways, and what follows are some examples of the most popular therapies.

Eye Movement Desensitization and Reprocessing Therapy

Eye movement desensitization and reprocessing (EMDR) incorporates elements of cognitive behavioral therapy with eye movements or other forms of rhythmic, left-right stimulation, such as hand taps or sounds. These work by "unfreezing" the brain's information processing system, which is interrupted in times of extreme stress.

EMDR is one of the most tried-and-true methods of unlocking and releasing trauma, even though the method may sound like an idea some mad scientist thought up. But for many people, it is a tremendous, near-miraculous help.

Francine Shapiro, Ph.D., pioneered EMDR, a form of psychotherapy. EMDR uses bilateral stimulation of the brain through the movement of the eyes, sound, or touch to help process trauma. By alternating the stimulation of both sides of the body, this therapy helps a person with PTSD process trauma that is stored in the neural networks of the brain and body. It helps release the "charge" that keeps a memory of past wounds impacting the present.[22]

Here's a simplified metaphor—using the word picture of ice and a blender—that helped me grasp how EMDR works.

We all have regular, weekly (if not daily) fears or upsets (a driver who cuts us off, a rude coworker, a stubbed toe) that are like little chunks of ice that flow through our emotional brain and eventually get processed and dealt with in a healthy way. We can usually handle these upsets, especially if our brain is fairly balanced. Our

---

22 "History of EMDRIA," EMDR International Association, n.d., www
.emdria.org/displaycommon.cfm?an=1&subarticlenbr=3.

psyches process these ice chip–sized memories—melting them, chewing them, dissolving them, or redistributing them—and life returns to normal fairly quickly. It's our brain's way of helping us, in mafia-speak, "fuggedaboutit" and move on.

When we are hit with a tragedy or trauma, however, it's like being hit with a heavy block of ice rather than the little ice chips. It is too big for our brains to process normally. A big trauma blocks the brain's normal ability to process pain and release it out of the body.

Ultimately, EMDR works a bit like a high-powered blender. It breaks up the "ice block" of traumatic memory into manageable pieces so that they can flow through your psyche and out of your body without creating blockages in the area of the brain that tends to cling to looping, negative thoughts. To simplify even more, EMDR helps turn monster memories into medium-sized memories so they can go through the normal brain-drain system!

EMDR is especially helpful for people who have a trauma incident that haunts them in their daydreams and nightmares. If a horrible story keeps repeating itself in a dream when your loved one sleeps, EMDR is worth a try. A story has gotten stuck in her psyche. EMDR could help break it up so that the brain can process it out of her mind in the way we process other types of pain or shock.

Emotional Freedom Technique

Many therapists refer to the emotional freedom technique (EFT) as "tapping." This is a method that you can learn on your own or from a professional facilitator. EFT draws on some of the elements of both EMDR and acupuncture. To perform this technique, you or a practitioner can repeat a phrase while tapping your finger on certain pressure points on the body (like your temples or the soft part of your clavicle). Because trauma affects both the thinking and automatic body responses, techniques that both affect the brain and touch the body are often very effective for PTSD.[23] I'd recommend checking into and learning this technique just because it is easy, free, and gives you and your loved one a portable tool to use anytime, anywhere. Sometimes just having something methodical to do—anything!—gives us a feeling of control when we start to panic or feel ourselves detaching. It is also easy to teach kids.

Somatic Experiencing Technique

Dr. Peter A. Levine discovered the somatic experiencing technique, a method of helping people dislodge trauma that stores itself in the body. Dr. Levine observed how animals in nature handle trauma and drew some similarities with how human beings dislodge trauma from their bodies in healthy ways. He also studied the myriad ways trauma affects the body when it does not dissipate normally—from tension to overreaction to tics. When we have "trapped" trauma, we are like tightly wound coils of unreleased energy. A quick way to learn more about Dr. Levine's methods is to look at some of his introductory YouTube videos. Dr. Levine and many other professionals believe that it is important to treat any stored trauma in the body first so that the person with PTSD can then begin to process the mental trauma. If you've ever been in

---

23   You can learn more about EFT at Gary Craig, "The Gary Craig Official EFT Training Centers," n.d., www.emofree.com.

an accident or terrifying situation, you may recall that you weren't able to think, answer questions, or process what happened until you were first allowed to breathe and calm your body. In the same way, Dr. Levine feels that teaching a client with PTSD how to recognize his or her body's responses and how to release tension gradually should come before talk therapy. One method is to notice tension in your body (as you are remembering or sharing a traumatic event) and then exaggerate the tension by tightening those muscles up even more, then gradually releasing and relaxing them.

If talk therapy has not yielded results, many people find that a method that also engages the body is especially helpful in getting relief—often quickly.

Body Work

Dr. Bessel van der Kolk is a doctor, teacher, author, and one of the leading experts on treating trauma. His book *The Body Keeps the Score: Brain, Mind, and Body in the Treatment of Trauma* describes how trauma rearranges the brain's wiring—"specifically, areas dedicated to pleasure, engagement, control, and trust."[24] He shows how these areas can be reactivated using therapies like neurofeedback, mindfulness techniques, play, yoga, and medication and talk therapy.

Any kind of gentle movement exercise or healing touch therapy (such as therapeutic massage) can help release and relax the body and support PTSD healing.

---

24 "About Dr. Bessel van der Kolk," Trauma Center, accessed September 1, 2017, www.traumacenter.org/about/about_bessel.php.

Cognitive Behavioral Therapy

One of the most prevalent therapies that psychologists use for healing trauma is cognitive behavioral therapy (CBT). CBT is based on the premise that changing the way we think changes the way we behave. It's all about thought monitoring: learning to hear your own internal dialogue, recognizing when it's skewed, and intercepting bad thoughts and replacing them with more peaceful ones.

Therapists use CBT to direct patients to question their runaway thoughts and to replace them with calmer, happier ones that are just as true but less stressful. CBT is also great for keeping someone with PTSD in the now—in the moment—when his or her mind begins to drift off into dark places.

I think CBT is wonderful, but it may be most helpful after EMDR or another therapy that also incorporates body movements. CBT deals only with our thinking and is especially helpful when it comes to finding logical ways to look at past trauma and reframe it for a positive purpose.

Dialectical Behavior Therapy

Mental health professionals use dialectical behavior therapy (DBT), a subset of CBT, as a specific training course to teach their clients specific skills in an orderly way that helps change negative thoughts, beliefs, and behaviors. Therapists focus mainly on helping patients learn methods that will decrease emotion dysregulation, self-destructive behaviors, and other unhealthy coping mechanisms.

Here's one example of a DBT technique. It uses the acronym "ACCEPTS" to help a person distract herself from unpleasant emotions temporarily until she can get to help or a better place to unpack them and deal with them. Each letter stands for some self-soothing skill that the person with PTSD can use to distract herself from a negative looping thought that is causing emotional pain:

- *Activities.* Use positive activities that you enjoy.
- *Contribute.* Help others or your community.
- *Comparisons.* Compare yourself either to people who are less fortunate or to how you used to be when you were in a worse state.
- *Emotions (other).* Cause yourself to feel something different by provoking your sense of humor or happiness with corresponding activities.
- *Push away.* Put your situation on the back burner for a while. Put something else temporarily first in your mind.
- *Thoughts (other).* Force your mind to think about something else.
- *Sensations (other).* Do something that has an intense sensation that is different from what you are currently feeling, like taking a cold shower or eating a spicy candy.[25]

There are several systematic techniques like this that are taught by DBT professionals. This method is often taught in a group setting. I love DBT because it is so specific and easy to remember and practice.

---

25   "ACCEPTS," DBT Self Help, accessed September 1, 2017, www.dbtselfhelp .com/html/accepts.html.

Exposure Therapy

Therapists use exposure therapy as a method of desensitizing some-one to a trigger that has caused her fear or panic in the past. Mental health professionals call this *habituation*, a process that operates under the premise that if you expose people to the thing they fear while they are accompanied by a safe and comforting companion, the fear will lose its hold on them. In exposure therapy, therapists ask patients to confront, in a safe way, the very situations, objects, people, and memories they have attached to the trauma (and are probably very consciously avoiding). This technique works well for those who are, for example, too afraid to get back behind the wheel of a car after a traumatic accident or those who are afraid of flying after some sort of scare in the air.

Family Therapy

Because PTSD affects the whole family and not just one person, family therapy can help give everyone a voice in a safe place. No one person should be the single vortex around which everyone else lives their lives, and families should not have to feel like they are walking on eggshells to avoid triggering the one who has PTSD.

Medication

Doctors and therapists can recognize when it is appropriate to pre-scribe medication for people with out-of-control panic and anxiety related to PTSD. But it is best if this medication is used tempo-rarily or in conjunction with therapies that get to the root causes of PTSD and relieve the symptoms in lasting ways. For example, antiobsessive antidepressant medications are sometimes helpful in pausing the painful looping thoughts and memories that intrude upon sleep. But there are side effects, including some lethargy or mental fogginess (especially at first) and sexual impairment. And in some people, antidepressants may help for a while and then actually make things worse.

People with PTSD often suffer from some anxiety, but most antianxiety medications can lead to addiction. Alternative therapies that help calm an anxious brain may be more helpful in the long term. Remember, I think of my two cats as my living Prozac and Xanax because they make me slow down and breathe slowly several times a day as they seek attention and want to be petted. My anxiety has dropped tremendously since we got Sweet Pea and Rocco. "Pet two cats and call me in the morning" is often my best advice.

In summary, those with PTSD should use medication in the smallest dose for the shortest amount of time that is needed. I would highly recommend reading books or listening to CDs by Dr. Daniel Amen to get the most up-to-date brain health information on medications, supplements, and other alternatives to ease the symptoms of PTSD and any other co-occurring mood or sleep issues. There are some good medications, and many are lifesaving. But some can be hard on the brain and body and make things worse. So you want to proceed with caution, talk with your doctor, and collect a store of good information before just accepting a quick prescription.

CHAPTER NINE

Post-traumatic Growth

What does not kill me makes me stronger.

Nietzsche, *Twilight of the Idols*

Since the late 1990s and early 2000s, professionals in a branch of positive psychology have been interested in exploring the potential benefits of trauma by looking at those who survive a trauma and eventually thrive. The term post-traumatic growth, sometimes known as "benefit finding" or "post-stress growth," has given us a more hopeful way of looking at trauma and the process of healing from it. I absolutely love this area of study and the way it helps us reframe trauma into something productive, helpful, and life giving. The most amazing, authentic, brave, fun, and compassionate people I know have all been through some sort of major crisis or trauma and have come out the other side of it changed for the better. Think of the people you admire the most. The ones who inspire you. The ones who love you and encourage you and show an abundance of empathy. Were they just born this way? Most of them, I'd venture to guess, have been through stuff. Hard stuff—painful stuff. The kind of stuff that buckles the knees and leaves you feeling as lost and disoriented as a child for a while. But somehow, they found their way through. And once they made it to the other side, they were different: more real, kinder, more loving, more compassionate, and perhaps even happier and more at peace.

This, I believe, can be anyone's story, no matter how great the loss or severe the trauma. The human spirit plus God's grace can lead us to glorious freedom of mind and heart. We become wonderful, messy, and beautiful wounded healers.

Researchers suggest that between 30 and 70 percent of people who experience trauma also report positive change and growth coming out of the traumatic experience. People who have gone through PTSD to the stage of post-traumatic growth experience several benefits. First, their self-concept changes after discovering their own hidden strengths when facing a traumatic challenge. They have a greater sense of personal resiliency and wisdom, perhaps coupled with a greater acceptance of their vulnerabilities and limitations. Second, they discover who their true friends are. After I went through a period of deep loss and trauma, I found which friends would stay by my side, come what may. Many people come out of trauma valuing their friends and family more, with a greater sense of compassion and desire to help others in the same way they were helped by compassionate people. Finally, trauma is one way that our philosophies and viewpoints can change—sometimes radically so. Many feel a fresh appreciation for life and understand what really matters at a deeper level.

More Vulnerable, but More Capable

Those who experience post-traumatic stress are illustrative of a great paradox: their losses have given rise to valuable personal gains. Another paradox is that people may feel more vulnerable post-trauma yet stronger. They realize that terrible things can happen to any of us, but they also understand that they are stronger than they thought and that the human spirit will fight back from despair and loss and eventually find its way to peace again.

People who move from PTSD to post-traumatic growth share several qualities or experiences. First, they must learn to overcome feeling helpless. Any therapies or thoughts that help them feel less like a victim and more like a victor or overcomer are significantly helpful. Second, they need to attach some meaning to their loss and recovery. This is where someone who is a spiritual director, pastor, or Christian counselor can help. Deep questions like "Where was God when I was hurting?" need to be asked, explored, and tended to without making our loved one feel guilty. For example, Philip Yancey's book *Where Is God When It Hurts?* (2010) has comforted thousands. Third, people who go from trauma-induced stress to trauma-induced growth find or regain their sense of optimism. This happens as they begin to see benefits of overcoming hardships and pain, and the glass starts to appear half full instead of half empty again. Finally, they create a nurturing social network that supports, cheers on, and encourages their growth after loss.

Telling New Stories[26]

We live in a world where bad stories are told, stories that teach us life doesn't mean anything and that humanity has no great purpose.

---

26 Some of the material in this section is adapted from my book *Nourished: A Search for Health, Happiness, and a Full Night's Sleep*, written with my daughter Rachel Randolph. (See Suggested Resources section for more information.)

It's a good calling, then, to speak a better story. How brightly a better story shines. How easily the world looks to it in wonder. How grateful we are to hear these stories, and how happy it makes us to repeat them.

Donald Miller, *A Million Miles in a Thousand Years*

One way the brain processes upsetting information or events is through telling itself stories from different angles until it settles on a narrative that fits and best helps us move forward. It's vital to question the stories we tell ourselves. If these looping stories continually bring up painful emotions of anger, resentment, worry, or sorrow, we need to search for some better stories. If we cling to stories that flood our bodies with toxic emotions, they can take us on a one-way trip to despair and bitterness. Oftentimes, it's not the actual event or person that wounded us that keeps on hurting; it's our thoughts about the event or person that hurt so much. Others may have hurt us once, but by rumination, we reinjure ourselves again and again.

Jesus spent much of His ministry undoing false stories and replacing them with truer, better ones. The Sermon on the Mount is a great case in point. There, He began each thought with "You have heard it said, but I say unto you" so that He was, in essence, introducing fresh twists on old ways of looking at life. When we exchange false, painful stories for God's truer, better ones, we also change our emotions, our moods, our personalities, and the outcome of our very lives over time. I have seen this concept at work when two different people experience the same kind of loss or hurt, but they let that loss shape them in two very different ways. They have the same injury, but the crucial difference is that one chose a "grievance story" while the other chose a "nourishing story."

A fabulous example of this is my friend Shawn. We've known each other since our teenage years. She found the love of her life in midlife, but she and Ron were married just five years before he died of complications in surgery. Shawn was devastated and grieved his loss profoundly. Within a couple of years, however, she met a widower whose name was also Ron. Happiness returned. They married, and she moved to his country home in Alabama. He provided Shawn with her own version of Eden: a patch of pretty tree-covered land, a garden, a cozy house with a wide front porch, and dogs. Lots of dogs. Two of her adult children soon moved nearby as well, which delighted her heart. Shawn and her children found solace and fresh hope in the happy, healing surroundings that her second husband provided.

But after just a few years, Ron was diagnosed with pancreatic cancer and died within a few weeks. Two husbands, both named Ron, both gone within five years of marriage. Shawn would be the perfect candidate for growing bitter at God and giving up on life and love and hope. However, one day, she wrote me the following email, and I knew my brave friend would find a way to rise above even this sorrow:

> As I look back, I see a row of soil just like in my garden. All kinds of seeds are being dropped into the groove of earth: some good, some bad. Right behind them are these big manly, powerful hands gently covering each seed with rich, warm, healthy soil and patting

it down to perfection. That's what God does. He doesn't stop the bad stuff from happening, but he covers it up with good things and then most likely waters it with His own tears.

Losing my first husband Ron was a horrible thing. God covered it with Ron's invitation to join him in Alabama and become his wife. My adult daughter moved nearby, and her life has been changed forever, her marriage on track, her health restored. My lastborn Evan, was taken from a scattered life with no future to live near us and find a career and start a family. Jack-Henry, Evan's new son, was created from the entire situation. Only a good and loving God could accomplish those things.

Now I feel like I'm observing another "bad seed" being planted; and only God knows what good things He is conjuring to cover it up with.[27]

Shawn could have so easily told herself stories about God's unfairness and grown sad, ugly, and bitter. Instead, she prayed and asked Him for a better, truer story. And indeed, God gave her a nourishing word picture of healing and hope. This is a fabulous, classic example of a person moving from post-traumatic stress into post-traumatic growth simply by changing the way she looked at tragedy and at God.

---

27   This quote and story adapted from *Nourished* (224–25). Email content from Shawn Shupe Mahan, personal communication, 2013.

Let Go of Controlling Anything or Anyone … except for Your Thoughts

Trauma teaches us, with renewed clarity, that we cannot control life, other people, or most circumstances. We are not in charge of much at all, really, in this world. God allows us control *over just one area of our lives*, and that is … we get to choose our thoughts about what happens to us and how we will respond. We get this privileged choice almost every second of every day of our lives. It is no small gift. We can cocreate with God in new ways to process what happens to us, totally changing our experience of it. It will not happen without proactive effort, but if your beloved with PTSD is determined, with time and practice, she can change the way her brain processes old trauma, and she can improve the quality of the rest of her life.

It has been said that there are two kinds of pain. We feel clean pain when something hurts us, usually out of the blue. It's the big "initial ouch" and the normal fallout of a painful or traumatic event. Dirty pain is when we create ongoing "grievance stories" about what happened to us and then go over and over them in our minds, nursing grudges, staying stuck, and, therefore, continuing to reinjure ourselves with our painful thoughts long after the event has transpired. Though we often have no control over the trauma that happens to us, determining to do all we can to learn how to calm our psyches after trauma is under our control. Your loved one will complete the healing process more easily if he is able to reframe a victim story into one where he goes on to become the overcomer, the hero of his own story.

One way to do this is for your loved one to write out the loop-ing "victim story" that goes around in her head (or for you to listen as she tells it to you). Now have her "write her own ending," one where she goes from being a victim to using the traumatic event as a springboard to becoming a hero, a giver, a thriver in life. This is a powerful exercise. Once the new story is written, have your loved one read it again and again. Remind him of elements of his "hero story" when he rises above a PTSD trigger or uses his past pain to help empathize with someone else. Pain is a great motivator for change and for finding our callings in life.

The Power of Visual Metaphors

The mind thinks in pictures, so when you can visualize a story or a word picture, the brain can latch onto an abstract concept much easier. The brain in pain is already struggling to function, so if you can link to a mental image that doesn't require a lot of thought, it may be particularly soothing. Some people love the image of Jesus asleep in the boat amid a terrific storm. He had not one worry and was just snoozing away. When He woke up and saw the commo-tion, He calmly said, "Peace, be still." Waves, thunder, and the fast-beating hearts of the frightened men—all became instantly calm. When I am afraid, I like to visualize the scene of Jesus sleeping in the boat, and I sometimes imagine that I'm tucked in His arms, where there is no fear no matter how the storm rages.

I believe the twenty-third Psalm is so beloved by people in grief or pain because of the rich word pictures it creates: a kind and comforting shepherd leads His beloved lamb through the darkness, making sure that this hurting lamb gets to rest in green valleys and that her thirst is quenched by a pool of blue water. For those who have felt the sting of betrayal, the picture of Jesus Himself preparing a table and a feast just for you "in the presence of my enemies" (Ps. 23) is one that reminds you that God sees you, values you, and honors you, no matter what others around you may think.

I have often asked God to show me a healing image that will calm my runaway mind, and He has always been faithful. The word pictures often come from biblical stories, but sometimes they are simpler and more concrete.

One day, I saw a lazy Susan with bowls spaced evenly on the turning table. For me, it became an image of God putting a bowl in front of me that was filled with my tasks for the day. The other bowls were filled with tasks for other days, and God would turn the lazy Susan and put those in front of me when it was time for me to deal with them. If I were to reach into other bowls meant for other days, I would only make a big mess. It was a simple picture, but it helped me stop trying to do everything all at once; to ask God, "What's in my bowl today?"; and to focus on accomplishing just those things.

In closing this book, I would like to share a blog post from a dear friend of mine, author Tricia Lott Williford. She wrote two beautiful memoirs about the tragedy and trauma that occurred in her life when her husband died suddenly and unexpectedly just two days before Christmas. At the time, their little boys were ages three and five. *Shock. Trauma. Grief. Heartache*—all words we use to describe great loss and sorrow, but truly, words do not capture the emotions. They are too big for words to contain.

A few years later, however, Tricia met Peter in a love story you can read for yourself on her wonderful blog. They married this past summer in perhaps the happiest ceremony I have ever seen. The bride was radiant. The groom was over the moon. And her two sons were ecstatic.

Joy. Fun. Play. Laughter—beautiful words and beautiful emotions cascaded like a happy waterfall back into Tricia's life.

Then December came. And with it, some surprising feelings. Tricia has survived a great trauma, and PTSD is part of her story for now. I'll let her tell the rest.

Trauma, Triggers, and Marriage: Hello, December
Posted on December 12, 2016

I'm going along, minding my own business, creating this new and beautiful life just the way I want it to be, and suddenly it's December.

There we are, singing Christmas songs in the car, and suddenly I need to change the station. There are holiday scents in the air, some variety of cinnamon, and suddenly I feel like I need to leave the room. We are singing together at choir rehearsal, and suddenly I'm crying and crying and crying. We are watching the last two minutes of the last episode of *This Is Us*, and suddenly I'm tied in the knots of a wordless, seizing panic attack.

It all happened so suddenly.

Which made me mad, because I don't want to be undone over Christmas anymore. I want only happiness now. It's a new season. God has done great things, given me everything I asked for, restored my joy and turned my mourning into dancing. I'm happy now. And I want to be happy at Christmas too. But there I was, in an emotional setback that I didn't want, an emotional setback that Peter didn't know what to do with.

It seems that I skipped the sadness last year. I was pretty hopped up on limerence, as you might recall. Last year's brand new love was the drug that carried me over the moon, and it kept me, quite frankly, distracted from the December cloud of the last five years.

So when it showed up this year, when I felt the anxiety mounting and the darkness looming, I didn't know what to do.

I feel crazy in love with Peter, but why was last December easy and this one is hard? I mean, nobody can maintain that kind of craziness that comes with the weeks of falling in love. It's not sustainable. It's replaced with the comfortable space of knowing and being, which is wonderful and comfortable ... and a safe place for grief to return.

Sometimes I don't want this story to be my story anymore.

The return of December has put me back in Jana's office. This time, Peter came too, since this isn't just mine anymore. Actually, marriage means none of this is a "His or Hers" kind of thing anymore. For better or for worse, this is Ours.

We're learning a whole lot over here. Just in case you love somebody who is triggered by things you can't understand, we've decided to share our list with you.

Emotional Memory Is Different from Logical Memory. There are things you choose to remember because it's a logical connection. Like when you see someone wearing a blue shirt, and it reminds you of your roommate's blue shirt that you borrowed for that one date ... and you intentionally follow a rabbit trail to that memory. That's a logical memory. But emotional memory is different. You might see the blue shirt, have no logical memory of the blue shirt, and somehow you just feel sad. It may be perhaps because a paramedic's uniform was that color of blue, and it's a peripheral memory that only registers as sadness. Emotional memory is hard to trace; it's involuntary and it only produces ... well, emotion.

Emotional Memory Is the Result of Senses. The scent of a candle. A song on the radio. Christmas lights on the drive home. They trigger emotions.

All of This Is Not Surprising. December is filled with scents, smells, sounds, and songs. And so of course this is happening. I cannot will it away. These are deep neurological paths that I'm trying to fight, and that is no small thing.

All of This Is Also Unpredictable. Sure, it would make sense for me to slip into a spiral closer to December 22, December 23 … but the first day of December? Where did that come from, three weeks early? Triggers are unpredictable, and they are in charge.

I Didn't Ask for These Triggers. I'd prefer to not have them at all, thanks.

Trauma Isn't Longing. These episodes that send me spinning are about Trauma. That is all. These episodes are not about indulging in a memory, and they are not about my longing for a different life or an earlier husband. I don't wish for anything to be different about this beautiful life of mine; this cannot be overstated.

Trauma Isn't Logical. So You Can't Explain a Traumatized Person Out of It. In case you're thinking, "But you had thirty good Christmases before that one bad one … can't you just think about a different one?" Well, all I can say is, no. I can't. It doesn't work that way.

Some Things Can't Be Fixed; They Can Only Be Carried. As Peter said, "I don't have to fix it. I only have to be available to my wife."

My Emotions Don't Have to Rule the Day. Peter said, "Honey, I love you and I am in this with you. But with all due respect to your story and what you've been through, Christmas isn't sad for me. And I won't give up my happiness this season." It's possible to read that and hear insensitivity; but the truth is, this is a very healthy response that is every opposite of codependent. Plus, there's so much comfort in knowing I can feel how I feel without ruining Christmas. Peter is holding on to his joy, and I love him so much for the consistency he brings and the light that he shines in this shadow.

I asked Peter what he would say to a fellow person in the support role. He said, "I would tell them to remember this isn't about them. It's an opportunity to not be selfish. This season gives me a chance to love somebody more than I love myself. So, if you're married to somebody who's struggling, then get over what you wish this looked like, and support this person who wishes it looked differently, too."

In case you love somebody who has triggers of PTSD, in case you're in love with somebody who's emotionally undone for reasons that are deeper than logic and longer than a season:

Please buckle up, stay close, and love us anyway.[28]

---

28   Tricia Lott Williford, "Trauma, Triggers, and Marriage: Hello, December," *Tricia Lott Williford* (blog), December 12, 2016, www.tricialottwilliford.com/2016/12/trauma-triggers-marriage-hello-december/.

I can think of no better way to close this book than to echo my friend's words to those who love someone with PTSD: "Please buckle up, stay close, and love us anyway."

It is my prayer that this book might give you some practical ways to do all three of those things.

Suggested Resources

Supportive Literature

American Psychiatric Association. *Diagnostic and Statistical Manual of Mental Disorders*, 5th ed. Arlington, VA: American Psychiatric Publishing, 2013.

Aron, Elaine. *The Highly Sensitive Person*. New York: Citadel, 1996.

Cushatt, Michele. *Undone: Making Peace with an Imperfect Life*. Grand Rapids, MI: Zondervan, 2015.

Klinic Community Health Care. *The Trauma-Informed Toolkit*, 2nd ed. Winnipeg, Manitoba: Klinic Community Health Care. http://trauma-informed.ca/wp-content/uploads/2013/10/Trauma-informed_Toolkit.pdf.

Lambert, Kelly. *Lifting Depression: A Neuroscientist's Hands-On Approach to Activating Your Brain's Healing Power*. New York: Basic Books, 2010.

O'Connor, Lindsey. *The Long Awakening*. Grand Rapids, MI: Revell, 2013.

Orloff, Judith. *Emotional Freedom: Liberate Yourself from Negative Emotions and Transform Your Life*. New York: Three Rivers Press, 2011.

Schiraldi, Glenn R. *Post-traumatic Stress Disorder Sourcebook*. New York: McGraw Hill, 2009.

Williford, Tricia Lott. *And Life Comes Back*. Colorado Springs: Waterbrook, 2014.

———. *Let's Pretend We're Normal*. Colorado Springs: Waterbrook, 2015.

Wolfelt, Alan. *Reframing PTSD as Traumatic Grief*. Fort Collins, CO: Companion Press, 2014. www.centerforloss.com.

Yancey, Philip. *Where Is God When It Hurts?* Grand Rapids, MI: Zondervan, 2010.

Zayfert, Claudia, and Jason C. Deviva. *When Someone You Love Suffers from Posttraumatic Stress*. New York: Guilford Press, 2011.

PTSD and the Body-Brain Connection
Levine, Peter A. *Trauma and Memory: Brain and Body in a Search for the Living Past; A Practical Guide for Understanding and Working with Traumatic Memory*. New York: Penguin Random House, 2015.

van der Kolk, Bessel. *The Body Keeps the Score: Brain, Mind, and Body in the Healing of Trauma*, reprint ed. New York: Penguin, 2015.

For Survivors of Childhood Abuse and Neglect
Schwartz, Arielle. *The Complex PTSD Workbook: A Mind-Body Approach to Regaining Emotional Control and Becoming Whole*. Foreword by Jim Knipe. Berkeley, CA: Althea Press, 2017.

For Soldiers and Public Safety Personnel (Christian Perspective)

Adsit, Chris. *The Combat Trauma Healing Manual: Christ-Centered Solutions for Combat Trauma*, 1st ed. Charleston, SC: Book-Surge, 2007.

Mumford, Nigel. *After the Trauma the Battle Begins*. Albany, NY: Troy Book Makers, 2011.

For Survivors of Sexual Abuse (Christian Perspective)

Allender, Dan B. *The Wounded Heart: Hope for Adult Victims of Childhood Sexual Abuse*. Colorado Springs: NavPress, 2008.

Langberg, Diane Mandt. *On the Threshold of Hope: Opening the Door to Healing for Survivors of Sexual Abuse*. AACC Counseling Library Series. Carol Stream, IL: Tyndale House, 1999.

EMDR

Shapiro, Francine. *EMDR: The Breakthrough "Eye Movement" Therapy for Overcoming Anxiety, Stress, and Trauma*. New York: Basic Books, 1998.

———. *Getting Past Your Past: Take Control of Your Life with Self-Help Techniques from EMDR Therapy*. Emmaus, PA: Rodale Books, 2013.

Preventing PTSD in Kids

Levine, Peter A., and Maggie Kline. *Trauma-Proofing Your Kids: A Parents' Guide for Instilling Confidence, Joy and Resilience*. Berkeley, CA: North Atlantic Books, 2014.

Self-Care Support for Companions of Those with PTSD

Henslin, Earl, with Becky Johnson. *This Is Your Brain on Joy*. Nashville, TN: Thomas Nelson, 2011.

Johnson, Becky, and Rachel Randolph. *Nourished: A Search for Health, Happiness, and a Full Night's Sleep*. Grand Rapids, MI: Zondervan, 2015.

Audio Recordings

Mumford, Nigel. *Relaxation and Healing Prayer*. http://byhis woundsministry.org/product/cd-relaxation-healing-prayer/.

Websites

www.giftfromwithin.org—Full-service website with articles, books, and audio and video recordings (Also includes recommended therapists for both those with PTSD and their caregivers or support people.)

www.emofree.com—Information about EFT

www.maketheconnection.net—Information and resources for veterans with PTSD and their families

http://menshatteringthesilence.blogspot.com/—Online support group for men who have suffered childhood sexual abuse, by Cecil Murphy (Supportive books by Murphy also found here.)

www.militarywithptsd.com—Resources for military with PTSD and those who love them

Online Support Groups

Anxiety Disorder Association of America offers online forums as
well as self-help information

Daily Strength provides online PTSD peer support groups

HealthyPlace PTSD forums

Mental Health of America provides online PTSD information for
the general public and veterans specifically

National Alliance on Mental Illness provides support and programs

National Center for PTSD provides online PTSD information for
the general public and veterans specifically

PTSD forums provide online PTSD peer support groups

PTSD Service Pets

http://therapypet.org

www.pawsforveterans.com

www.soldiersbestfriend.org

www.usserviceanimals.org

NEWLIFE | Help in Life's Hardest Places

Talking about the things no one else will, to bring healing to those who've lost hope

"*I have been living with my secrets* for 30 plus years while failing time and again to stop and all the while them getting worse. For the first time I have learned more about why it is happening, developing an action plan to change, and creating a network of support."

— Jack
Intensive Workshop attendee

NEW LIFE MINISTRIES EXISTS TO GO INTO LIFE'S HARDEST PLACES *with you.*

800-HELP-4-ME
NewLife.com

When you or someone you love is in crisis, you need a trusted friend to walk alongside you—a helper who's been there and understands, but who also has the training and skill to offer practical help.

New Life Ministries, founded by Steve Arterburn, exists to go into life's hardest places with you.

For over 30 years, we've provided expert answers to people just like you on our call-in radio show, *New Life Live!* We also offer a host of other resources, Intensive Workshops, and referrals to a carefully selected network of counselors.

Visit NewLife.com today to see how we can help, or call 800-HELP-4-ME. We want to hear from you!

About New Life Ministries

New Life Ministries, founded by Stephen Arterburn, began in 1988 as New Life Treatment Centers. New Life's nationally broadcast radio program, *New Life Live!*, began in early 1995. The Women of Faith conferences, also founded by Stephen Arterburn, began in 1996. New Life's Counselor Network was formed in 2000, and https://tv.newlife.com/, the ministry's Internet-based television channel, was launched in 2014. New Life continues to develop and expand their programs and resources to help meet the changing needs of their callers and listeners.

Today, New Life Ministries is a nationally recognized, faith-based broadcasting and counseling nonprofit organization that provides ministry through radio, TV, their counseling network, workshops, and support groups, as well as through their numerous print, audio, and video resources. All New Life resources are based on God's truth and help those who are hurting find and build connections and experience life transformation.

The *New Life Live!* radio program, still the centerpiece of the ministry, is broadcast on Christian radio stations in more than 150 markets. It can also be seen on several network and online channels.

New Life's mission is to reach out compassionately to those seeking emotional and spiritual health and healing for God's glory. New Life Ministries Resource Center receives thousands of calls each month from those looking for help.

For more information, visit newlife.com.

About Stephen Arterburn

Stephen Arterburn, M.Ed., is the founder and chairman of New Life Ministries and host of the number-one nationally syndicated Christian counseling talk show, *New Life Live!*, heard and watched by more than two million people each week on nearly two hundred stations nationwide. He is also the host of New Life TV, a web-based channel dedicated to transforming lives through God's truth, and he also serves as a teaching pastor in Indianapolis, Indiana.

Stephen is an internationally recognized public speaker and has been featured on national media venues such as *Oprah, Inside Edition, Good Morning America, CNN Live*, and *ABC World News Tonight*; in the *New York Times, USA Today, US News and World Report*; and even in *GQ* and *Rolling Stone* magazines. Stephen has spoken at major events for the National Center for Fathering, American Association of Christian Counselors, Promise Keepers Canada, the Lifewell Conference in Australia, and the Salvation Army, to name a few.

He is the bestselling author of books such as *Every Man's Battle* and *Healing Is a Choice*. With more than eight million books in print, Stephen has been writing about God's transformational truth since 1984. His ministry focuses on identifying and compassionately responding to the needs of those seeking healing and restoration through God's truth. Along with Dr. Dave Stoop, he edited and produced the number-one-bestselling *Life Recovery Bible*.

Stephen has degrees from Baylor University and the University of North Texas, as well as two honorary doctorates, and is currently completing his doctoral studies in Christian counseling. He resides with his family in Fishers, Indiana.

Stephen Arterburn can be contacted directly at SArterburn @newlife.com.

About Becky Johnson

Becky has authored or coauthored over fifty books in her twenty-five years as a writer, covering everything from family humor to relationship improvement to brain science!

Her recent titles include coauthored books with Dr. Earl Henslin (*This Is Your Brain on Joy* and *This Is Your Brain in Love*, both with Thomas Nelson), her daughter Rachel Randolph (*We Laugh, We Cry, We Cook* and *Nourished: A Search for Health, Happiness, and a Full Night's Sleep*, both with Zondervan), and Steve and Misty Arterburn (*The Mediterranean Love Plan* [Zondervan, 2017]). She has also worked as a professional writer and research assistant with pioneer brain expert Dr. Daniel Amen for his blog and his book *Use Your Brain to Change Your Age*.

Along with writing and enjoying her roles as wife, mom, and grandmother of seven, Becky enjoys sharing the antics of her two cats, Sweet Pea and Rocco, on social media; going thrifting, upcycling, and selling vintage items on Etsy; and whipping up culinary creations for her family and friends. She has a food blog at www.laughcrycook.com.

At David C Cook, we equip the local church around the corner and around the globe to make disciples. Come see how we are working together—go to **www.davidccook.com**. Thank you!